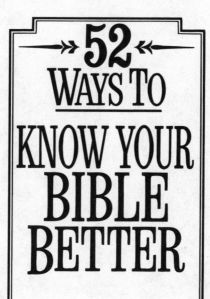

52
WAYS TO
KNOW YOUR
BIBLE
BETTER

»52« WAYS TO KNOW YOUR BIBLE BETTER

Robert Jon Crown

OLIVER NELSON

THOMAS NELSON PUBLISHERS
Nashville

Published in Nashville, Tennessee, by Oliver-Nelson Books, a division of
Thomas Nelson, Inc., Publishers, and distributed in Canada by Lawson
Falle, Ltd., Cambridge, Ontario.

Unless otherwise noted, the Bible version used in this publication is THE
NEW KING JAMES VERSION. Copyright © 1979, 1980, 1982, Thomas
Nelson, Inc., Publishers. Scripture quotations marked NIV are taken from
the HOLY BIBLE: NEW INTERNATIONAL VERSION. Copyright © 1973,
1978, 1984 by the International Bible Society. Used by permission of
Zondervan Bible Publishers.

Printed in the United States of America.

Crown, Robert Jon.
    52 ways to know your Bible better / Robert Jon Crown.
        p.   cm.
    ISBN 0-8407-9618-8 (pbk.)
    1. Bible—Study and teaching.   I. Title.   II. Title: Fifty-two ways to
know your Bible better.
BS600.2.C68   1992
220′.07—dc20   92-14599
                                                              CIP

1   2   3   4   5   6   —   97   96   95   94   93   92

Contents

KEY QUESTIONS TO ASK YOURSELF

EXPLORING THE BREADTH AND DEPTH OF THE BIBLE'S MEANING

▪ Introduction

T he Bible is like no other book you have ever read. It is actually a series of books written over several centuries by many authors writing primarily in two ancient languages. It is written in a number of literary styles, with books of varying length and emphasis on different subjects. Still, that isn't what makes the Bible different.

What sets the Bible apart is its one continuous theme—a thread that runs from cover to cover: God is, God creates, and God desires a relationship with His highest creation, the human race.

All of the books of the Bible point toward that central theme. Many lesser themes and principles run parallel. There is unity in the thought of the Bible, even though the voices and stories are diverse. The symbols run true from cover to cover. The New Testament fulfills the Old in countless ways. The words of the prophets come to pass. The Bible's teachings fit together layer upon layer upon layer—or, as the Scriptures say of themselves, "precept upon precept, line upon line, here a little, there a little"—each passage showing us another facet of the same brilliant gemstone.

The Bible is, indeed, the Book of books. It is

God's Word to humankind. It reflects God's nature. It expresses His truths, His will, His commandments, His blessings and judgments, His thoughts and feelings toward human beings and, above all, His love.

The Bible has life-giving value. It nourishes the soul and causes the spirit within to grow and to become strong. It reveals Jesus by the Spirit of truth, and the more you experience Jesus, the more sensitive and intuitive your thinking will become in spiritual matters.

The power of the Word makes us whole. It balances us, heals us, restores us, and pulls us together as fully integrated, fully alive human beings. This life-giving value extends through eternity. The Word of God prepares us for our eternal home with our heavenly Father and enables us to arrive at heaven's gate with joy in our souls and victory in our hands. It is through the Word that we gain the ability to endure anything that the enemy of our souls may launch against us.

52 Ways to Know Your Bible Better offers suggestions about how to read the Bible to gain the most from it. Consider it an introduction to your search of the Scriptures. It has been written to help you know God's Word better, recognizing fully that anytime you read the Bible with an open heart and active faith, you truly become a little more like God's Son, Jesus, who is the living Word.

GETTING
STARTED

1. Know the Author

The Bible is a spiritual book. The mind alone cannot fully comprehend it. As much as you may be familiar with the history, facts, and literary qualities of the Bible, you will never grasp the deep meanings of God's Word through your intellect.

How can we truly begin to understand the depths, riches, and fullness of God's Word?

One Message By knowing the Author of the book! We can personally know God the Father, God the Son, and God the Holy Spirit. The Lord Jesus Christ came to earth to make that possible. He died for our sins, was resurrected, and is alive today. The Bible says "the Word became flesh." Jesus existed before the world was created, and the Scriptures say that by Him, in Him, and through Him all things were made. His life and the written words of the Bible exist in perfect harmony; they are one message.

Invite Him into Your Life The first step in knowing Jesus is to invite Him to share your life —to come into your spirit and to cleanse any area that is displeasing to Him. Part of that invitation must be a commitment to having an ongoing relationship with God: to follow His Word, to talk with Him, to obey Him, to worship Him with other believers, and to serve Him in every avenue of your life.

Once you have invited Jesus into your life, you have His Spirit within you. The Bible, too, is imbued with God's Spirit. Thus, when your spirit is united with God's Holy Spirit, you are in a position both to know God and to understand His Book.

You can know people who know Jesus—who walk and talk with Him daily. You can meet Him briefly at church, and you can even read what He has said. A relationship with Jesus, however, is one in which He lives with you all the time and is invited into every area of your life. That is the beginning of knowing the Lord Jesus Christ.

The more you know Jesus—by communicating with Him daily and inviting His presence into every decision, every difficulty, every moment of joy —the more you will understand His Word. Conversely, the more you read your Bible, the more you will understand Jesus. With every hour of reading, you'll have new insights into what Jesus has said, done, and promised.

Delight in the Word   The more you know your Bible and its Author, our Lord Jesus Christ, the more you will love them both. Your appreciation for the Scriptures will go beyond awareness to awe, beyond information to inspiration, beyond knowledge to heartfelt desire and a delight in the commandments of God. You will hunger and thirst for the Bible because your spirit recognizes that it is being nourished each time you delve into the Scriptures.

Make a Decision If you have never made a decision to unite your life with Jesus, I invite you to make that decision today. Ask Him to come into your life, to cleanse all those areas that cause you guilt, anxiety, and fear, and to become the Lord— or ruler—of your life.

Simply speak to Him. Recognize that God is the almighty Creator and Jesus' sacrifice of death on the cross is the payment of sin. Ask Jesus to forgive you. Ask God to remove anything in your life that displeases Him. Ask the Holy Spirit to infuse your spirit, to live with you and lead you into all truth. Then commit to living your life pleasing to your Creator.

The Lord Jesus will look beyond the words of your prayer to your intentions, your will, and the meaning behind your words. He has promised that when anyone calls out to Him with a deep, sincere desire, He will respond.

Deepen Your Relationship If you already have a relationship with Jesus, make a commitment today to deepen that relationship. Renew your vows to the Lord. Ask Him to help you understand His Word and apply it to your needs.

2. A Firm Foundation

God does not change. He is immutable. He is absolute. He is the same "yesterday, today, and forever" (Heb. 13:8). He can always be trusted.

The Book that God has written—through inspired men from Moses in Genesis to the apostle John in Revelation—bears the same qualities. It is immutable. It does not change with the shifts of time, politics, or culture. The principles of the Bible are alive and as fresh and meaningful for us today as for those who first heard them centuries ago. The Word of God alone bears eternal spiritual absolutes.

Build on the Foundation   The Bible provides a foundation on which you can build your life so that it will withstand any onslaught—physical, material, relational, emotional, spiritual. Jesus says of His Word: "Heaven and earth will pass away, but My words will by no means pass away" (Luke 21:33).

When all else is passed away, only two things will live in eternity: God's Word and those of us who believe it. God's Word is eternal, and we who trust in the Lord Jesus are promised eternal life.

As you get acquainted with your Bible, you will

discover it to be a treasure chest of valuable, eternal, and absolute truth. When you regard the Bible as God's absolute eternal truth, you will undoubtedly

- approach what you read with greater seriousness. The Bible must command your attention and respect. Don't approach it as just "another good book." In so doing, you'll vastly shortchange its impact on your life.
- place greater value on your time spent reading God's Word and upon God's Word itself.

Put It to the Test Do you doubt whether God's Word is absolute or true? Test what you read against the broad scope of history. God invites you to do so. The Bible is filled with historical records of incidents in which God's people trusted His Word and succeeded or turned their backs on His Word and failed. The Scriptures continually challenge us to "inquire diligently," to "test," to "prove," to find "evidence" for believing. David wrote, "Oh, taste and see that the LORD is good; blessed is the man who trusts in Him" (Ps. 34:8). God's Word stands up to the test!

The next time you open your Bible, expect to encounter lasting truth. The Bible doesn't provide *a* way to live. It provides *the* way to live, now and forever, in God's loving presence.

3 ▪ Apply His Word

As you read your Bible, expect the principles you encounter to be true for you. The people in Bible times were human. They had the same desires and temptations, the same hopes and fears, and similar sorrows, pain, and needs. God's Word pinpoints your need with a description or example, and it also provides a course of action to follow.

So often, it's easy to read the Bible and think that it contains stories about another people, place, or time. The spiritual fact is that the Bible's stories could apply to today in New York or Nebraska!

Personal Application It isn't enough to read and believe the absolute principle of God: "You shall not steal." You must say to yourself, *I* shall not steal. This commandment is for me personally. It tells how I should live.

Knowing it's wrong to steal (whether taking scissors from work, cheating on taxes, or swiping England's crown jewels) and "not stealing" are two different things. You must follow through and do what you know to do, and *not* do what you know is contrary to God's highest desires for you. That's when God's Word becomes reality.

The more you apply the Bible's principles to

your life—not just in recognizing that they do apply but in actually living out the principles in your life—the more you will trust the Bible. And the more you will trust God's Word to be true in its entirety. Your faith continues to build as you take God's Word into your life and begin to live it. You then have firsthand knowledge that God's Word works.

4. Ask the Holy Spirit to Be Your Teacher

Jesus promised His disciples, "The Helper, the Holy Spirit, whom the Father will send in My name, He will teach you all things, and bring to your remembrance all things that I said to you" (John 14:26).

The Holy Spirit is our supreme Bible teacher today. He is the One who quickens the Bible to our minds, causes it to sink deep within our spirits, and secures it as part of our lives forevermore.

Before You Begin   Before you begin to read the Bible, pray,

Father God, I ask You please to send the Holy Spirit, to cause my mind to be open to all that You want to reveal to me in this passage. Teach me, Holy Spirit. I ask this in the name of Jesus. Amen.

While You Read   If you are having difficulty understanding what you are reading or if you are having difficulty concentrating, stop to pray,

Heavenly Father, I need the Holy Spirit to help me concentrate on what I am reading. Turn my heart solely toward You and Your words to me today.

Take away the scales from my spiritual eyes and help me to see what You have for me to see in Your Word. I trust You to do this as I pray in Jesus' name, Amen.

After You Read After you have finished reading a passage, pray,

Father God, I ask the Holy Spirit to help me see how this passage fits into the entirety of Your Word. Cause me to assimilate what I have just read and to incorporate it into the greater understanding that I am developing about the Bible as a whole. Help me to remember what I have just read and to be aware of ways in which I can use this information today and in the future. I pray in the name of Jesus, Amen.

Have confidence as you pray that the Holy Spirit wants you to understand the Word. He desires for you to learn and to be all that you can be in Christ Jesus. You will always be praying fully within the will of heaven when you pray,

Lord, help me to become more like You and to know Your words and trust them for my needs.

AMEN!

GETTING ACQUAINTED WITH THE BOOK OF BOOKS

5. Getting the Layout of the Land

When the children of Israel neared the borders of the Promised Land, Moses sent in ten men to "spy out the land" (Num. 13). If you are not familiar with the contents of the Bible, you need to embark on a similar reconnaisance mission.

Note How the Bible Is Put Together
Thumb through the Bible from cover to cover. The Bible has sixty-six books—thirty-nine in the Old Testament (the Hebrew Scriptures), followed by twenty-seven in the New Testament (the Christian Scriptures). Within each book, the content has been divided into numbered chapters and then into numbered passages called verses. When the Bible was written originally, the chapter and verse designations were not part of the manuscript. These were added later to make it easier for us to locate and refer to specific passages. Thus, we say John 3:16 rather than "about a seventh of the way through the gospel of John." John 3:16 is shorthand for the third chapter of the gospel of John and the sixteenth verse.

Note "Helps" in Your Bible   Your edition of the Bible may have one or more of the following:

- *Concordance or a Bible cyclopedia (or both).* These helps locate specific passages according to a word or theme. For example, if you want to read Bible passages that include the word *hope,* look up *hope* in the concordance. Cyclopedic references usually relate to a person, place, or broad subject, such as forgiveness, peace, or love.
- *Maps.* You can study various journeys in the Bible and see how the political divisions of the Bible lands have changed through the years. You can chart out the original boundaries God chose for the Israelites and recognize that He has kept His promise in bringing them back to His land.
- *Charts and tables.* Bible helps often include timelines, comparative lists (for example, the miracles and parables of Jesus as they are repeated in the four Gospels), or tables of comparative weights and measures as well as money conversion tables.
- *Bible study guides or commentaries.* Outlines and Bible study notes may appear at the back of the volume or may be interspersed in the text. Such material is also frequently located at the beginning of each book—for example, facts about the book's contents, its author, the audience to which it was written, key con-

cepts and verses in the book, and ways to study the book.

Note Special Treatment of the Text Itself

Some words may be printed in red; these are the words of Jesus. Some passages may be highlighted or marked in a special way; these are frequently passages for which a commentary has been provided elsewhere. Other Bible references may be in small type at the end of verses; these are verses elsewhere in the Bible that are related to the passage. This use of related Scriptures is often called a chain reference or cross-reference. Notice, too, any subheads that the Bible publisher has provided (these are not a part of the original manuscript of the Bible).

In some Bibles, such as the Amplified Version, words are put in parentheses or brackets. Again, these words were not a part of the original manuscript but are supplied by the version writer or translator to give a more complete meaning in English. Italicized words in most texts have been added to the original translation for greater understanding in English.

You need to be aware, at the outset, that the Bible is the most intriguing, wonderful, and multifaceted book you are ever going to read. Spy out the land!

6. Old and New— Hebrew and Christian

Both Testaments are for us today. Nothing in the New Testament negates the truth or value of the Old; nothing in the Old Testament precludes or eliminates the need for Jesus to be our living Savior and Lord. It has been said, "The Old Testament is the New Testament concealed, and the New Testament is the Old Testament revealed."

The disciples of Jesus wrote the New Testament. Nearly all were Jews who knew and believed the Old Testament; the apostle Paul was especially knowledgeable.

The Bible was written over a period of fifteen hundred years—beginning with an oral tradition in which the stories were told and retold verbatim from generation to generation.

The Old Testament   The Old Testament— the Hebrew Scriptures, the covenant established between God and His chosen people, the children of Israel—has five main sections. These are divisions according to content, not divisions you will find within the manuscript.

The first five books are referred to as Torah or the Law. These books are attributed to Moses. They tell about creation, the first generations on the earth, the call of Abraham and the promises made to him, the story of the descendants of Abraham, the deliverance of God's people from slavery in Egypt, and the commandments, ways and means of worship, and rules that God established for His people as they wandered in the wilderness on their way to the Promised Land.

The next group of books tells the history of God's people in the Promised Land. Included are personal stories about individuals: Ruth, Esther, and Job.

Psalms is the "songbook" of the Bible. If you open your Bible in half, you'll generally find yourself in Psalms. Music or praise and worship have always been central to our faith as God's people!

Proverbs, Ecclesiastes, and the Song of Solomon are called the Wisdom Literature. These books vividly detail our love relationship with God and our fellow human beings.

The final seventeen books of the Old Testament are the writings of the prophets. Isaiah, Jeremiah, Daniel, and Ezekiel are commonly called the Major Prophets. The Minor Prophets are no less major in importance; rather, "minor" applies to the length of their messages.

The New Testament   The New Testament —the Christian Scriptures, the covenant based on the sacrifice of Jesus on the cross—has four main sections. The first four books are called the Gospels—Matthew, Mark, Luke, and John. They tell about the life of Jesus from four different viewpoints. The word *gospel* literally means "good news." Jesus came to bring the good news of God's love for us.

Following the Gospels is the Acts of the Apostles, which gives the history of the early church, including the mission trips and key sermons of Peter and Paul.

Next come the Epistles—a series of letters to the first believers as they were scattered throughout the Roman Empire. These are informational, inspirational, corrective letters directly from the apostles.

Finally, we have the book of Revelation. It was written by John, an apostle of Jesus, shortly before John's death while he was a prisoner in exile. He foretells what he sees as the future of the church and the ages.

The Whole Counsel

One of the apostle Paul's chief arguments in defense of the faith was this: "I have not shunned to declare to you the whole counsel of God" (Acts 20:27). A repeated admonition in God's Word is to avail ourselves of "the whole truth," "the complete gospel," "the entire word"—the whole counsel. As you read the Bible, you'll find that the counsel of the First Covenant enhances that of the Last Covenant. The message of the Bible must be taken as a whole.

7 ▪ Choose a Version That You Can Understand

We are privileged to have a number of translations and versions of the Bible available to us. No other people in the history of the world has had such ready access to the Bible.

The first English translation of the New Testament was printed in 1525, and it was 1535 before the entire Bible was published. Prior to that, Bibles were handwritten—a tedious process that took years for completion. The Word of God was rare, owned only by royalty or by the church. Most people could hear it read only during church services, generally once a week.

Translations and Paraphrases　　A translation of the Bible is, technically speaking, one that has been created by scholars who have referred to ancient manuscripts in the languages in which the Bible was written originally—Hebrew for the Old Testament, Aramaic or Greek for the New—and who have subsequently translated the ancient languages into English.

A paraphrase, in contrast, is created by someone who refers to an existing English translation and attempts to update the words and phraseology into language more readily understood today. Paraphrases have not been published to tamper with or diminish the original texts of the Bible but to enlarge the readership.

The most widely published translation of the Bible is the King James Version—the manuscript that King James authorized for official use in England. It was published in 1611.

Among the most widely circulated translations today, in addition to the King James Version, are these:

- The New King James Version (an updated version)
- The New International Version
- The New Revised Standard Version
- Today's English Version (Good News)

The most popular paraphrases include these:

- The Living Bible
- The Amplified Version

Choose the Version You Enjoy Reading You may want to choose a paraphrased Bible as you begin your adventure in Bible reading. If you don't understand the Bible you presently own, buy a new one. Plan to spend as much as an hour in your local Bible bookstore making your selection. Choose one chapter—perhaps a chapter in the gospel of John—and read that in several versions. Which one is the easiest for you to understand? Take that one home with you . . . and read it!

8 ■ Begin with the Gospels

Begin reading the gospel of Matthew. It's easy to find as the first book of the New Testament. But you may want to skip to the second or third chapter. The first chapter is mostly genealogy, listing the ancestors of Jesus. The second chapter is the Christmas story. (If it's not Christmas, you may want to get directly into the adult life and ministry of Jesus, and come back and read the Christmas story at a later time.)

After Matthew, read directly through the rest of the Gospels: Mark, Luke, and John. Mark and Luke repeat many of the stories, events, and teachings in Matthew. The gospel of John was written after the other three Gospels. Matthew, Mark, and Luke tell what Jesus said and did. John tells who Jesus was and is from the standpoint of heaven and eternity.

Read Acts Next   See how the followers of Jesus took what He said and did, and acted upon it. See how the church began. See the message and miracles that gave birth to the faith we have today.

Reread   And then, go back and read the Gospels and the book of Acts a second time. We read our favorite books a second time and see our favorite movies again and again. The same principle works here. You'll get a lot more out of the Gospels and the book of Acts the second time through.

Turn to the Old Testament   Start with Psalms and Proverbs. You'll find it easy to relate to the wide range of emotions in the Psalms.

Explore   And then branch out. The Bible contains the most action-packed, intriguing true stories in all the world—and with a valuable glimpse of who God is and how He works. Always keep bookmarks in the Gospels, Acts, Psalms, and Proverbs so you can return often to your favorite messages of God's love and deliverance.

Take Heart!   The more you read the Bible, the more connections you'll be able to make from book to book and passage to passage.

9. Ten-Minute Readings

Ten-minute reading is a discipline you can make and keep for the rest of your life. Give it a try. You'll be amazed at your growth by the end of one year. After all, by reading the Bible faithfully for ten minutes a day, every day for a year, you'll have spent more than sixty hours reading the Bible. Imagine how much better you'd know any subject after sixty hours of focused reading.

Advantages Choosing to read the Bible at least ten minutes a day has two noteworthy advantages:

1. You Can Always Find Ten Minutes Ten minutes can be carved out of virtually any person's day:

- Sitting in a lobby as you wait for an appointment or the arrival of a client
- Waiting to board your plane
- Taking a coffee break
- Waiting for the fish to strike

2. Many Educators Consider Ten Minutes to Be the Ideal Length for a "Learning Period"

Virtually any concept—even the most complicated scientific material—can be broken down into short, readily learned subunits. The same is true for the Bible. By concentrating on one segment of the Bible—and limiting yourself only to that segment during a specific period of time—you will probably find yourself more readily able to absorb that information and comprehend it.

Feed the Inner You   Consider your ten-minute reading time to be a mealtime for your inner person. The Bible proclaims, "Oh, taste and see that the LORD is good" (Ps. 34:8). You will probably devote one or more hours today to the feeding of your physical, perishable body. Choose to devote at least ten minutes to the nourishment of your everlasting, imperishable soul and spirit.

You'll probably find that there will be times when you want to read fifteen minutes or longer. There will even be times when you want to feast on the Word for several hours or all day. You may find that you desire to have several ten-minute reading times throughout the day.

Honor Your Commitment   If you miss a day of ten-minute reading, don't feel that you need to compensate for it by reading twenty minutes the next day or allow yourself to go on a guilt trip that will keep you from the inspiration of the Bible for several more days. Just pick up your commitment again the next day and read for ten minutes.

PRACTICAL
SUGGESTIONS

10 ■ Read It Fresh!

No matter how many times you've read the Bible, you'll always find something fresh and new in it. That's one of the great, awesome mysteries about God's Word. As Lamentations 3:22–23 declares, God's "compassions fail not. They are new every morning." So, too, are the insights into God's Word at each reading.

How can you find something new in a passage that you know well, even by memory? How can you find living meaning in a passage that has always seemed dull?

1. Read the Passage Aloud Slowly   Often, we rush through those passages with which we are familiar. Try slowing down and listening to yourself read each word.

2. Take a Look at Each Word   Concentrate on each word or phrase. Ask yourself questions about it; let your mind be open to new meanings. Consider the opening line of the Lord's Prayer: "Our Father in heaven, hallowed be Your name" (Matt. 6:9).

- *Our* Ask yourself, Why doesn't it say *my* Father? What does it mean to be part of the family of God? What does it mean to have the same spiritual Father that Jesus has?

- *Father* Meditate on the fact of God's fatherhood. What does it mean for Him to be our Father? What privileges and responsibilities are His as Father? What is our role, and blessing, as children?

- *In heaven* What does it mean that God has an exquisite place, an abode, a headquarters from which He controls the universe? What is my hope that I will one day be with Him there? What is my concept of heaven?

- *Hallowed (or holy)* What does it mean for God's name to be hallowed? Have I heard His name used in vain today? How do we hallow His name? (You may even want to look up the word *hallow* in a dictionary.)

Take a look at each word of some favorite Bible verses. Compare different versions for word derivations. You'll find a multitude of new meanings and insights.

3. Ask the Holy Spirit to Reveal New Meaning or Insight into the Passage   This step is especially appropriate for those passages that you may not have enjoyed reading previously. Many times we allow ourselves to skip over certain passages because we have not considered them important or pertinent, or perhaps we once heard a sermon on the passage that left us uninformed, uninspired, or unnerved.

At other times, we don't want to face the discipline our hearts feel at reading a passage of Scripture. As we mature—grow "to the measure of the stature of the fullness of Christ" (Eph. 4:13)—we welcome these times when we feel correction from the Scriptures. Through experience, we come to know the joy of sins forgiven, the freedom of living without bitterness, the peace that pervades us when we have no hidden agendas. May we desire continually to experience His unlimited love for us so that with renewed hearts, we will count on the Holy Spirit for inspiration from the Word as it establishes, settles, and strengthens us. (See 1 Pet. 5:10.)

Ask the Lord to give you fresh insight into a too-familiar or too-much-ignored passage before you read it. Pray,

Why, Lord, did You put this in here for me? What can I learn from it? How can I apply this to my life? What more is there for me to glean from this part of Your Word?

Trust the Lord to be your good Shepherd, who makes you to "lie down in green pastures" where your soul can be fed (Ps. 23:2).

11 ▪ Read the Word First Thing in the Morning

Most nutritionists consider breakfast the most important meal of the day. A well-balanced breakfast gives a person quick energy in the morning and sustaining strength for early afternoon.

Many creative people point to the early morning as their most productive time. The first thoughts are often the freshest, most innovative ones. In the early morning, the mind is receptive to new ideas, unburdened by the day's worries, uncluttered by the day's agenda and problems.

Spiritual Food   What is true for the body and mind is also true for the spirit. The morning hours are prime ones for your soul. Awaken your spirit with praise! Nourish it with spiritual food. Read your Bible as part of your morning routine. Add it to your existing schedule just as you include getting dressed and listening to the news. In fact, make it your first priority.

When we eat breakfast, we rarely see the connection between the foods we take in and the agenda before us. We eat for the total well-being of the body, trusting that the energy and strength we receive from the food will be sufficient for whatever physical demands are placed upon us throughout the first part of the day.

The same is true for the Bible. We may not see a direct connection between what we read and the tasks before us. Still, whatever we read from God's Word nourishes the soul and provides the spiritual fuel we need to withstand the wiles of the devil, follow through on what the Holy Spirit compels us to do and say, pray for those in need, and rejoice in the Lord always—in all situations.

"Seek First the Kingdom"   Many workers listen to the Bible each morning on cassette tape as they drive to the office. They arrive ready to face the day.

Don't turn to the Bible as a horoscope or as a predictor of your day. Don't expect every verse to provide overwhelming direction for the decisions you will face in any twenty-four-hour period. Rather, expect the Word of God to mold your soul. You become adept in a subject area or a skill after years of training and experience. You become physically fit after months of eating and exercising in proper balance. You will become more spiritually fit and wise as you read your Bible with regularity day in and day out, month after month, year after year.

Begin your day in God's Word. The rest of your day will flow more smoothly. And if troubles arise as a flood, you'll have strength to navigate the rapids!

12. Read the Scriptures Aloud

When you read the Scriptures aloud, more of your senses are called into play than when you read with your eyes alone. You actually take in more of God's Word. Your comprehension of the passage and your ability to recall it are both enhanced significantly.

Reading aloud also forces you to concentrate with greater intensity. The mind is less apt to wander if the mouth reads the words that the eyes see.

Spiritual Renewal   Apart from what happens to you intellectually as you read aloud, something mysteriously wonderful happens to you spiritually. Your faith is built up in a way that seems uniquely related to hearing. Romans 10:17 tells us, "Faith comes by hearing, and hearing by the word of God."

Try walking the floor today, reading your Bible as you carry it before you. A foremost evangelist of our day tells how he, as a teenager, read the Bible to the trees as he walked in the woods near his parents' home. Wherever you are, the unseen host of heaven will delight in hearing God's Word coming from your lips!

Reading the Scriptures aloud also causes you to recognize more of the power inherent in God's Word. It is a power to convict and bring about change—in yourself and in the lives of others.

The Old Testament records several instances in which kings and prophets insisted that the Word of God be read aloud to all the people. The result was always the same: the people were moved to repentance, and they experienced deep spiritual renewal.

Special Passages   Certain passages are especially worthy to be read aloud.

- Read aloud the teachings of Jesus, especially His parables and the Sermon on the Mount (Matt. 5—7). Jesus never wrote a book or a letter, as far as we know. He spoke His message to the people, saying, "Those who have ears to hear, let them hear." Jesus invites us today to hear His words, both literally and figuratively.
- Read aloud the sermons of Peter to the crowd on the day of Pentecost (Acts 2:14–36), to the Sanhedrin after the healing of a lame man (Acts 4:8–20), and to the house of Cornelius (Acts 10:23–43).
- Read aloud the sermon of Stephen, the first Christian martyr (Acts 7).
- Read aloud the discourses of Paul before Felix and Agrippa (Acts 24—25).
- Read aloud the message of King David (2

Sam. 22) and the sermon of King Solomon (2 Chron. 6).

- Read aloud the letters of Paul, Peter, James, and John to the churches (Rom.; 1 and 2 Cor.; Gal.; Eph.; Phil.; Col.; 1 and 2 Pet.; 1, 2, and 3 John; James; and Hebrews).

  These letters were written to churches established by the apostles in various cities throughout the Roman Empire. The letters were read aloud in the churches so that all could hear them.

- Read aloud or sing the Psalms (perhaps to your own tune). The Psalms were written as songs meant to be heard. Reading them aloud can become an act of prayer, praise, and worship.

Don't let the strangeness of some words and names bog you down. Pronounce the words as best you can and move forward. Read with authority and fire as if you are determined to keep your soul awake. You'll likely succeed.

13 ∎ Read and Reread

One of the greatest advantages that came with the printing of the Bible was that laypersons could read and reread the Bible at their own pace, at their own timing, and at their own choice of passage. Many a Christian was martyred for that privilege. Don't let their shed blood be in vain.

Read and reread God's passage until you experience meaning from it. In rereading God's Word— literally washing your soul with it again and again —you begin to experience the real life-changing and cleansing power of the Bible.

Your Understanding In rereading a passage—over years or repeatedly in a short period of time—you accomplish the following:

- Focus attention on one passage until you reach the point of comprehension and gain a new understanding of God's meaning.
- Experience new insights into how a passage might be applied to your life.
- Commit the passage to memory, lodging it deeply within your soul where it can never be destroyed or stolen.
- Have ready access to God's truth so that you

might apply it freely in a crisis situation or share it with a person in need.

Your Pace It doesn't matter, ultimately, how fast you read the Bible or how often or how many chapters you read in a single sitting. What matters is that you walk away from each reading experience with a better understanding of how God desires for you to live on this earth in order to experience more of His love and blessings. What you gain in spiritual meaning is all that really counts. Therefore, if you need to read one verse ten times before moving on to the next verse, do so! That's your privilege.

You'll never be given a test or a timed exercise on the Bible (unless you seek one). You're not accountable to any other person on earth for what you know about God's Word (unless you choose to be). Eternity will reveal what you have learned and how well you have applied the Bible to your soul. That gives you great freedom as well as great personal responsibility to read slowly . . . read deeply . . . and read repeatedly.

14 ▪ Make Notes

The Word of God is sacred. It is living and un-changeable. The printed words on the bound vol-ume that you hold in your hands, however, are there only for you to use in learning the Word of God.

As you read your Bible, mark it up. Have a pen or pencil handy. (Certain highlighters don't bleed through Bible-quality paper.) Keep a notepad nearby.

Underline It   Underline passages that hold particular meaning for you. Circle words that prick your interest. Write in the margins. Use your Bible as you would use a textbook that you own—mak-ing your notes at the tops and bottoms of pages to help you remember where to find passages special to you.

Date It   At times, certain passages will seem to provide an answer for you or be a signpost giv-ing you direction in a specific situation or be a promise to you about your future. Mark those pas-sages and date them (including the year). If the passage relates to someone else, or if it relates to a certain need or circumstance, you may want to add a few words of description along with the date. When you review your Bible in the years ahead, these passages will have special meaning for you.

List It   Many Bibles have several blank pages at the back. Feel free to use them for notes or lists.

For example, you could do an in-depth study of the fruit of the Spirit given in Galatians 5:22–23. List the traits—love, joy, peace, longsuffering, kindness, goodness, faithfulness, gentleness, and self-control—on a page in the back of the Bible. As you read, you will likely discover passages that relate directly to one or more of these traits. Write the references in the back of the Bible, too. At year's end, you will have enough information for a Bible study course on the fruitful life of the Spirit.

One man has written the names of his wife and children in the back of his Bible. As he reads the Word, he frequently encounters verses that seem to leap out at him in relation to a family member. He notes those verses next to the name of the person involved, providing a few words of description. In his Christmas letter to each family member, he shares the precious gift of God's promises that he has read and prayed for that person.

Over time, the worn, well-marked pages of your Bible will reflect your spiritual journey as no other document can.

15 · Consider the Stories as a Whole

In your reading, avoid the tendency to get bogged down in details. Read the stories in the Bible as you would read a newspaper or a letter written to you personally. Take in the whole of the message.

The Big Picture   Read five or six verses and stop. Ask yourself, What did this say? What is the story being told? Can I retell what I have just read? If not . . . reread the passage . . . read the passage aloud . . . relax! Many people become so uptight about reading the Bible that they actually shut off their ability to comprehend. They work at it too hard, trying to get meaning out of each word before they have grasped the bigger picture of the story.

Some of the best stories to read as a whole are in the Old Testament. These are the stories that many people recall hearing as a child:

- Adam and Eve in the Garden of Eden (Gen. 2—4)
- Noah and the ark (Gen. 6—9)
- Joseph and the coat of many colors (Gen. 37—48)
- Baby Moses spared (Exod. 1:15—2:10)

- Moses and the burning bush (Exod. 3)
- Moses and the crossing of the Red Sea (Exod. 13—14)
- Joshua and the battle of Jericho (Josh. 6)
- Gideon's defeat of the Midianites (Judg. 6—7)
- David and the defeat of Goliath (1 Sam. 17)
- Elijah and the widow of Zarephath (1 Kings 17)
- Elijah defeating the prophets of Baal (1 Kings 18)
- Elijah taken to heaven in a fiery chariot (2 Kings 2)
- The miracles of Elisha (2 Kings 3—8:6)
- Shadrach, Meshach, and Abed-Nego and Nebuchadnezzar's fiery furnace (Dan. 3)
- Daniel and the lions' den (Dan. 6)
- Jonah and the great fish (Jon. 1—3)

Dramatic Impact   Each story has as much drama in it as the latest suspense movie! In fact, as you begin reading, you probably won't want to stop when the story does.

The same holds true for the Acts of the Apostles. This book about the faith in action of the early Christians reads like a true-life drama.

The Bible has something for every reader—love stories, war stories, mysteries, political intrigue, pomp and circumstance, family conflicts of all types, life-and-death struggles, mighty miracles.

16 ▪ Study a Children's Version of the Bible

A good way to become familiar with the stories and teachings of the Bible is to purchase a children's Bible or Bible storybook. This approach is especially helpful if you have never read the Bible before. Start where children start.

Enjoy the Pictures Purchase the most beautiful children's Bible or Bible storybook that you can find. Delight in the illustrations! Plant the images in your mind. They'll help you understand the stories, just as they help a child. They'll also become an easily recalled point of reference for you later.

Work with a Child You may want to introduce a child to the Bible as you introduce yourself to the stories. Don't feel as if you have to answer all of the child's questions or know more about the Bible than he does. If the child asks you a question you can't answer, you can always say, "I don't know. Let's keep reading to see what we can find out. God knows everything, and we can trust Him to lead us."

Obtain Other Helps   Many children's Bibles have study helps—brief commentary passages, anecdotal illustrations, maps, and other reference materials. Some provide pronunciation help and definitions for key words and concepts.

In addition to a children's Bible, you may want to purchase a children's Bible dictionary or a set of Bible storybooks (akin to an encyclopedia). Excellent Bible-based videos make the stories come alive.

Other reference books that will be helpful as you explore the meaning of the Bible include:

- A concordance—*Cruden's, Young's,* or *Strong's*
- *Nave's Topical Bible*
- A Bible dictionary—perhaps *Nelson's Illustrated Bible Dictionary*
- *Manners and Customs of Bible Times* by Ralph Gower
- Bible commentary sets, such as those by William Barclay or Matthew Henry

Listen to Children's Insights   Invite children who visit in your home to read a story to you from your children's Bible materials. They'll learn, even as you do. Discuss the stories with them.

17 ∎ Take Your Bible with You to Church

Even if it isn't the custom in your denomination to do so, you should feel free to take your Bible with you to church or Sunday school.

Read Along   As various passages are read from the pulpit or lectern, read along in your Bible. Note the context by seeing what comes before and after the verses.

While the minister gives the sermon, mark up the passage in your Bible that is being used as a reference. Circle key words. Write comments in the margins. You may want to keep a few sheets of blank paper in your Bible for making additional notes. (Onionskin paper is great for this purpose!)

During the service, you may recall certain passages of Scripture that you have read during the previous week, or you may experience new insights into their meaning. Make a note in your Bible. Or you may feel inspired in a special way by a song that the choir or a featured music group sings, by the liturgy of the Communion service, or by a dramatic presentation made before the sermon. Again, make a note in your Bible.

Follow along in your Bible as your Sunday

school teacher explains a passage. You'll get more from the lesson.

Before-the-Service   Meditation   Time

Think about arriving a half hour before the Sunday morning worship service begins and sitting quietly in the sanctuary to read your Bible. Begin with the scheduled lessons for the service; also read a few verses before and after each passage so that you will have an understanding of the context. You may have time before the service begins to read through the hymns scheduled. This quiet time of meditation before the service will prepare your heart for the service and will likely give you new insights into the Lord's nature and His Word.

Take your Bible with you to church. Use it there, and mature progressively each week in your spirit.

18. Listen to Bible Tapes

Do you enjoy listening to tapes more than reading? Then listen to Bible tapes!

A number of excellent tape sets have been produced. Some are dramatized, with sound effects and multiple voices. Some have commentary materials or prayers interspersed periodically. Various versions of the Bible are available.

On the Road and at Home   Play your tapes of the Bible

- as you drive to and from work. Even if your commute is only fifteen minutes, you'll gain much by hearing the Word of God instead of the morning traffic reports and commercials. And if you get stuck in traffic, what better way to redeem the time than by listening to words that have eternal value!
- at home as you are gardening or making home repairs.
- in your bedroom before you fall asleep.
- in your kitchen as you are preparing meals.
- in your bathroom as you are shaving or taking a bath. (Position the player so that it can't

fall into the water, and keep electrical cords far away from the tub.)

- as you travel by car on a family vacation. Tapes provide one way to have a family devotional time. They frequently spawn conversations about the Lord and can lend an atmosphere of relaxing peace to a vehicle full of rambunctious or tired children.

Lend an Ear   Don't feel as if you need to concentrate on every word spoken on the tape. Play Bible tapes as you would background music. Occasionally, a verse will stand out to you. At other times, you'll find yourself repeating a phrase or verse just as you would a line from a song. The Word of God will become embedded in your spirit; your spiritual ears are often listening even if you are not conscious of the fact.

When our children were young, we frequently had Bible tapes playing when they brought their friends over. That led to conversations about the Bible and about the Lord. The tapes opened up opportunities to share the Lord with our neighbors and assisted our children in making our family Christian commitment known to their friends.

The Word of God is both soothing and invigorating. The commandments of God result in "length of days and long life and peace," and obedience to God's Word brings "health to your flesh, and strength to your bones" (Prov. 3:2,8). Surround yourself with the sound of life.

19. Keep a Bible-Reading Journal

A journal is ideal for recording prayer requests (and noting their answers), for writing down questions about God, your faith, and the Bible (and noting their answers), and for reflecting on passages of the Bible. And it allows you to look back at your growth in the Lord.

Keeping your study notes and reflections in a loose-leaf notebook has several advantages:

1. You can always pull out a page to take with you should you be asked to give a devotional or lead a Bible study.

2. You can readily add to your previous notes or reflections and still keep your materials in a page order.

3. You can easily collate materials according to topics or subheads for quick referral.

What types of things should you record in a journal?

Your Bible Study Notes   All of the studies mentioned later in this book can be recorded in your journal.

Your Reflections   Stop after you've read a book, a parable of Jesus, or an instructive passage and write freely (without being overly concerned about grammar, punctuation, or the organization of your thoughts) how you feel and respond to what you have read.

Your Inspirational Thoughts   Especially note those that come some time after you have read a passage—as a result of contemplation, a quickening of insight by the Holy Spirit, or a study of related materials that leads to a broader or deeper understanding of God's Word.

Your Synthesis of the Teachings of Others   Recall from memory what others have said or taught about God's Word and your response to their messages. Or you may take notes on sermons and put them into your journal, adding comments and Scriptures in the margins as the Holy Spirit quickens other insights to your mind.

Periodically take stock of your general spiritual growth, writing into your journal a "state of my soul" statement. Cite specific ways in which you believe you have grown, specific Bible studies you have completed and what they have meant to you, areas in which you feel you need to grow further, and subjects you want to explore in God's Word. Try to do this at least once a year.

20. Hide the Word in Your Heart

What you have hidden in your heart and mind is there for the Holy Spirit to quicken to your remembrance so that God's Word might protect you, comfort you, uplift you, strengthen you, calm you, instruct you, warn you, train you, and make you whole.

What you memorize of God's Word

- can never be taken from you. It is yours forever. Even when you are away from your Bible, the Word remains at your ready access.
- always goes with you. It is ready for you to share with others. And it will be with you through eternity.
- always is available for your meditation. You can experience new revelations and insights into God as you meditate upon His Word day and night.
- will be there in the deep recesses of your spirit even when you aren't consciously aware of it. What you memorize of God's Word provides a spirit-based rationale for quickly made, quickly needed decisions—including the formation of the motives underlying them.

As you learn more of your Bible, various portions will become so meaningful to you that you will never want them to be more than a few seconds from your ability to recall them. Those are the passages you should memorize.

Here are several suggestions as you commit God's Word to memory:

Always Memorize the Reference with the Verse (or Verses)   In other words, keep the "address" handy in your memory as well as the instruction or promise.

Memorization Is Actually Based on the Principle of Reading and Rereading Until You Are Reciting   As you memorize a verse, carry it with you or post it in a prominent place where you can look at it often. Educators tell us that we must repeat something at least seven times before we have it memorized.

Speak the Words Aloud   We memorize more by sound than sight. Talk the verse out repeatedly until you no longer need to refer to a printed version of it.

Memorize the Verse Accurately   Have someone "test" you.

Don't Try to Memorize Too Much at One Time
If the verse is a complex or long one, or if you are memorizing a passage of several verses or a chapter, commit one or two verses to memory each day. Add to your memory bank slowly. Most peo-

ple have difficulty memorizing more than twenty-five words at a time, and even segments that long should be broken down into smaller increments of seven to eight words.

Review and Rehearse What You Have Memorized in the Past   Periodically renew what you have committed to memory.

Memorize from the Version that You Read Most Often   Your mind will adopt a cadence as you read one version of the Bible over a period of time. A passage memorized from another version will seem foreign to your mind and lips. The King James Version has a poetic rhythm that makes it the easiest version for many people to memorize.

Challenge yourself. Ask the Spirit of truth to bring to your mind and then recite aloud from memory as many verses as possible.

21 ▪ Be Part of a Bible Study Group

Few activities are more rewarding and deeply fulfilling than studying the Word of God with others who love the Lord and are eager to learn what the Bible teaches.

Commit to a Group   Find a Bible study group in which you feel comfortable and make a commitment to it for at least a year. Such a group holds special advantages for you:

- It provides built-in discipline to read and study God's Word on a regular basis.
- It provides an opportunity to see the Word of God from other vantage points. You may not always agree with those in your group, but that's part of the growing experience a group study affords. You'll give and receive, teach and learn.
- It generally provides social times with other believers and opportunities to hear how other people apply the Bible to their lives. You'll discover the ways in which others have struggled in their Christian walk and how they have overcome obstacles.

Start Your Own Group   If you can't find a group that you can attend because of scheduling conflicts or one that is studying something of interest to you, consider starting your own Bible study group.

Before the Meeting

1. Choose a theme for the week—generally a single word or concept.

2. In a concordance, look up key Bible references on the theme. You'll need as many references as the number of people you expect to attend. Look up each verse. Some may address the issue or topic with greater potency than others.

3. Write each reference on a separate slip of paper, fold the paper, and put all of the slips in a box or bowl.

During the Meeting

1. Begin with prayer. Invite the Holy Spirit to be your teacher, and ask Him to lead you in your study.

2. Let each person pull a slip of paper from the bowl and look up the verse. Ask the members to spend several minutes in quiet contemplation on what they have selected; they may want to make a few notes. Suggest they read the surrounding verses in their Bibles to gain a more complete understanding of the context. (You may want to play a tape of praise music softly in the background.)

3. Invite each person to read the verse aloud (loudly, slowly, and clearly) and then to say two or

three sentences about what that verse means to him or her. Don't let the person ramble on.

4. After all of the verses have been read and shared, you may want to open up a general discussion about what you have read. Keep the discussion related to the Bible, and again, encourage participation by all.

5. Close the study time in prayer. Ask the Lord to help you remember what you have read and to let His Word sink deep into your heart where it will nourish your soul.

Always treat the Word of God with respect. In a group situation, don't allow the Word of God to be taken lightly. Cynicism can kill a Bible study. Have an agreement at the outset that you are approaching the Bible as God's Word to you. Choose to believe!

22. Teach the Bible to Children

Elementary-school-aged children will benefit from a Saturday morning enrichment program. Invite your children's friends to join you. For the areas in which you lack knowledge, ask other parents to come and teach the children.

Nations   You can study the nations of the world, with a special emphasis on the Bible lands. Use the Bible as a basic text as you delve into the history of the Middle East. Also study the Greek and Roman Empires and the way that the Christian faith spread across Europe and around the world.

Plants   You can focus on plants, including trees and flowers, both in your neighborhood and in the Bible. The children may want to design gardens (on paper) using only biblical trees and flowers. Look up references about biblical foliage—from roses to cedars to boxwood bushes.

Birds   The Bible speaks of buzzards, doves, eagles, falcons, hawks, partridges, pelicans, pigeons, quail, ravens, sparrows, storks, swallows, turtledoves, vultures, and more!

Animals   Explore the animal kingdom. Have discussions about camels, lions, bears, mice, rabbits, snakes, and so forth; read about animals from cover to cover in the Bible.

Insects   Extend your study to the insect world. Ants, bees, crickets, caterpillars, fleas, flies, gnats, grasshoppers, hornets, locusts, moths, spiders, and worms are all mentioned in the Bible.

Fish   Read New Testament stories related to the Sea of Galilee, the story of Jonah, and other references about fish.

Earth and Sea   Other areas to consider include the climate—clouds, rain, hail, storms, and the delicacy of snowflakes, each intricately and uniquely designed by the Creator—and things under the earth and sea—geology, gemstones, minerals, fossils, and archaeology. The basic reference material can come from God's Word.

The children will be fascinated by these courses of study. They will learn more about the Bible, and the teacher will learn most of all! The children will discover that the Bible is relevant to them and all the world around them.

23 ■ Relate the Bible to Your Children's Schoolwork

When you need to look something up, you probably go to the library or check dictionaries, encyclopedias, and other reference materials at home. Consult the family Bible at home too, especially as your children bring home school assignments related to science and social studies.

Solar System   Is one child studying the solar system? See what the Bible has to say about the sun, moon, and stars.

Anatomy   Is another child studying anatomy? Refer to what biblical writers have had to say about their own creation as physical beings. Look up *arm, leg,* and *hand.* See what the Bible has to say about the senses. Look up *eye, see, look, taste, hear, smell,* and *touch.*

Politics   Is your child studying political history? The stories of the Old Testament are filled with political intrigue.

Oceans   Is your child studying the oceans? See what the Bible has to say about sea creatures. Read about Paul's wreck in a storm off the island of Malta.

Music   Is your child studying music? Look up the names of specific instruments—such as *harp* and *cymbals*—as well as *music* and *singing*. Read about the great musical parade and celebration in 1 Chronicles 15—16.

Government and Current Events   Is your child studying government? Read what the Bible identifies as the hallmarks of a wise ruler and the marks of good leadership.

In your child's discussion of current events, refer to what the Bible has to say about various nations and issues. *See more suggestions in Chapter 39.*

Poetry   When your child begins to study poetry, suggest an examination of the poetry of the Bible. Many Bibles are typeset so that the poetry sections stand out.

As you and your children explore the Bible together in these ways, you'll gain an overview of the entire book.

24 ▪ Refer to a Daily Devotional Guide

Several million people faithfully read a devotional book or magazine on a daily basis: *The Upper Room, Daily Blessing, One Day at a Time, Forward Day by Day, Bible Pathway,* and so forth. Most of these daily devotional materials are based upon or include a Bible reference.

Procedure Find the reference associated with the Bible passage before reading the rest of the devotional, and then look it up and read it for yourself in your favorite Bible.

- Read several verses before and after the quoted passage to get it into context.
- Stop to dwell on the meaning of the passage. Can you apply it to your life?
- Compare your translation of the Bible with the one used by the devotional magazine. Note any differences that may expand your understanding of the verse or passage.
- Then, read what the devotional writer has to say.

In so doing, you'll gain much more from both the Scriptures and the devotional material. In essence, you'll be transforming the monologue that has been written to you into a dialogue. Your mind will naturally compare what you have read and contemplated with the material in the devotional book.

On some days, you may disagree with the devotional writer. Explore why. Can you relate your opinions directly to the Bible? On other days, you may say to yourself, Why didn't I see that? On still other days, your response may very well be, Isn't that interesting? What a good thought!

Types of Materials   Two types of daily reading materials are generally available: instructive and inspirational.

- *Instructive* materials often teach a book of the Bible, a subject-study course, or a sequence of lessons on a particular theme.
- *Inspirational* materials generally are based on references from various parts of the Bible, choosing verses for their uplifting, faith-building value.

Both types are useful. And both will help you know your Bible better.

25. Turn to the Bible First

In times of crisis, where do you turn first? What is your first response? On whom do you call?

Try the Bible!

Wisdom The Bible holds the collected wisdom of the ages for times like those you face daily, including crisis moments.

"But," you may say, "how can the Bible address the situation of a loss of data from my computer during a power surge?" By addressing how you feel and react to that situation.

The Bible doesn't address every situation known to human beings, but it does address every reaction a human being has toward situations with the environment, with other human beings, and with God.

Relationships Technology and customs may have changed, but human responses and emotions have not. The complexity of human relationships has remained unaltered through the centuries. Hurt, pain, despair, isolation and loneliness, depression, confusion, anger, sorrow, discouragement, doubt, bitterness, loss, frustration, fear—all of these reactions are reflected in the Bible. Many specific situations are also addressed: marital difficulties, birth, death, growing up, leaving home, sibling rivalries, accidents, competition, failure, violence, addiction, and many more.

Promises   Furthermore, the Bible offers countless promises for the believer that can be applied during crisis times—words of hope, faith, and love that buoy us up and carry us through life's tragedies.

As you face crises with your Bible in hand, you'll discover that the Bible way works. Your faith will be built up to trust God even more in the future. Your inner being will be strengthened.

Are you facing a crisis now? Turn to your Bible!

KEY QUESTIONS TO ASK YOURSELF

26 . What Does This Mean to Me?

As you read the Bible—especially passages of instruction, such as the parables and sermons of Jesus, the Epistles, and many of the prophetic messages in the Old Testament—ask yourself a two-part question:

What Does This Mean? Try to summarize the meaning of the passage in fifty words or less. Recall what you may have heard in sermons about the passage. Note the nouns in the passage. What do you know from your experience about these items? For example, if a verse refers to salt, light, fish, sand, rock, bread, road, robe, lake, ring, vineyard, or yoke, ask, What properties does this item have? What is this like? How and when is it used? Why would Jesus have chosen that item as an illustration?

Identify the verbs in the passage. What is the action in the passage? Consider the adjectives and adverbs.

Many of Jesus' teachings relate to farming. What do you know about plants and their growth? Are you a gardener? Did you grow up on a farm? To help you understand and apply the meaning of these passages, talk to someone who knows about farming. Ask specific questions.

If the passage mentions a place or name with which you are not familiar, look it up in a Bible dictionary. Locate it on a map. Something about the place may relate directly to the meaning of the passage.

You may want to consult a Bible commentary to discover what others have had to say about the passage. Get several viewpoints.

What Does This Mean to Me?   Ask yourself, How am I like the person in this story? If multiple characters are involved, ask yourself, With which character do I most closely identify? Ask, How did the people in this story feel? What did they think? Is there any event in my life that brought out those same thoughts and feelings?

The Bible wasn't written to confuse you. It was written to enlighten and instruct you! Ask the Holy Spirit to give you specific insights into what He wants you to know about a passage.

The apostle Paul wrote to the Ephesians, "I keep asking that the God of our Lord Jesus Christ, the glorious Father, may give you the Spirit of wisdom and revelation, so that you may know him better" (Eph. 1:17 NIV). Ask the Lord for specific wisdom and revelation.

27. Who Is Communicating?

As you read the instructive words of the Bible, ask yourself two closely related questions:

Who Is Speaking? Keep track of the voices in a narrative. In the parables of Jesus, note the central characters and what they have to say. Can you hear a tone of voice in their words? Try reading the passage aloud. Read it with several different inflections and tones of voice. Emphasize different words each time you read. What new levels of meaning have you uncovered?

Who Is Listening? Who is the audience? Had you lived in the time that the Bible story took place, would you have been part of the specific audience for a particular passage?

For example, ask yourself, Would I have been a Pharisee? Would I have washed Jesus' feet with my tears? Would I have followed Jesus out of town to sit on a hillside all day and hear Him speak? Would I, as a blind man, have cried out to Jesus as He passed by? Why, or why not?

Bear in mind as you read the parables of Jesus that at least two levels of communication are occurring simultaneously. There is the communication within the parable—character to character. And Jesus is telling the story to a specific audience for a specific purpose.

For example, in the parable of the good Samaritan, we find at least four characters, only one of whom speaks verbally. (The other three, arguably, could be said to have communicated by their behavior!) Many of us are familiar with this story about the man who is beaten and robbed. The actions of the priest and the Levite who ignore him as he lies wounded by the roadside convict us all. The Samaritan—considered a social outcast, a spiritually barren person—finally helps him. Do you know to whom Jesus was speaking when He gave this parable? See Luke 10:25–37 for the answer.

When reading the words of Jesus, always ask yourself, To whom was Jesus speaking? What was the response? How would I have responded had I been in their shoes?

In an even broader sense, we are the audience for *all* the words of the Bible. God is the speaker. We are the listeners. It's a good idea to stop periodically in reading and to pray,

I realize, heavenly Father, that it's no accident that I'm reading this passage today. There are no coincidences in Your design for my life. Lord, what are You trying to say to me right now? Lord, help me to have listening ears! In Jesus' name, I pray. Amen!

28 ▪ What Are the Human Feelings and Thoughts?

The Bible is a book about people. From cover to cover, we read about people and their relationships with one another and with God. As such, the Bible is a book about feelings and about the obedience and disobedience of men, women, and children to their Creator. When you read your Bible, try to isolate the feelings and thoughts of the speakers—both the characters in the stories and the authors of the books.

Feelings   What is the person in the passage feeling? Identify the central emotion, and then list the possible emotions. If the story has multiple characters, try to isolate the feelings for each one. Do the feelings shift during the story? Is there a difference in the way the people feel at the beginning of the story and at the end?

Thoughts   What do you perceive to be the thoughts behind the words that are spoken? What is the worldview of the speaker? The audience? What is the frame of reference?

In the parable of the prodigal son, Jesus tells of a

reprobate son, a faithful son, and a loving father (Luke 15:11–32). Identify and list the feelings and thoughts of each character at the start, in the middle, and at the conclusion of the story. Draw from your experiences in conjecturing what each may have felt.

Take a look at the feelings and thoughts you have identified. When have you had similar feelings and thoughts? Then return to the story and look for the central teaching of Jesus that addresses those feelings and thoughts.

Your Reaction   At other times, you may isolate the way you feel and think *after* you finish a passage. Have you just read a few verses that made you sad? Angry? Filled to overflowing with hope? Meditate on your response. Why are you feeling that way? What has triggered that emotion? Where else in the Bible do characters reflect this emotion? What did they do about it? What has God said about it?

Your reading of a passage in the Bible may trigger a string of seemingly unrelated thoughts. Pull them back into focus by asking yourself, Why does this passage cause me to think that way?

The Bible will evoke emotion in you. Allow that to happen. God created all humankind with a deep well of emotions. Explore those emotions in a positive way to grow spiritually.

29 ▪ What Is the Biblical Context?

More errors have probably been made in biblical interpretation as the result of one practice than all others combined: taking a verse out of context.

Psalm 139:17–18 declares,

> *How precious also are Your*
> *thoughts to me, O God!*
> *How great is the sum of them!*
> *If I should count them, they*
> *would be more in number than*
> *the sand.*

We need to take truth as the sands of the sea—as a whole, not as one or two isolated granules. Every verse in the Bible ultimately needs to be seen in the context of every other verse.

Work Toward the Goal   It follows that to see a passage in the fullness of the entire Bible, one must be familiar with the entire Bible. You can develop a sense of biblical context by doing the following:

- Read the verses immediately before and after the passage.

- Look up verses supplied as suggested cross-references or related passages.
- Consult an appropriate timeline. For the words of Jesus, consult a timeline of His ministry. (You may be able to find this among the "helps" in your Bible.) Is Jesus speaking at the beginning, middle, or final days of His ministry on the earth? In reading the Old Testament, you may want to consult a historical timeline. Several biblical authors were contemporaries. For example, Jeremiah, Ezekiel, Daniel, and Habakkuk were all contemporaries, living and writing in the sixth century B.C., and their writings are primarily related to the Babylonian exile of the Jewish people. The vital fact to us is that these truths are all relevant today. Prophetic writings are still being fulfilled.

Jesus' Example   Jesus said, "Beware of the leaven of the Pharisees" (Luke 12:1). Jesus also said, "To what shall I liken the kingdom of God? It is like leaven" (Luke 13:20–21). In the space of two chapters, He referred to leaven twice —with vastly different conclusions: beware; be like! One might be left with the question, Is leaven good or bad?

By reading the complete verses, however, one realizes that Jesus' admonition to "beware of the leaven of the Pharisees, which is hypocrisy" was part of a lengthier discourse on hypocrisy. When Jesus said that the kingdom of God was like leaven, "which a woman took and hid in three measures of meal till it was all leavened," He was teaching about the way in which the kingdom of God will expand and grow throughout the earth.

Overbearing Traits   As you read, be aware that these traits can keep us from pursuing the true context of any passage:

- *Our own prejudices.* We tend to see the Bible through the eyes of our past experience and societal and parental training, which may not have been according to biblical principles.
- *Our own sin.* We tend to justify those parts of the Bible that convict us the most deeply or make us uncomfortable.
- *Our own desires.* We tend to read what we want to read, with an emphasis on the promises of God and a deemphasis on the commandments.
- *Our past inaccurate interpretation.* We may have learned the Bible incorrectly. Let the Bible speak for itself, regardless of what others may have said that it says.

30. What Is the Historical Context?

In addition to recognizing the biblical context of a passage, we grow in our understanding as we become aware of its historical context. When you read the Bible, try to put yourself into the world as it existed in Bible times.

Consider the Way in Which People Lived No electricity. No rapid means of transportation. No immediate forms of communication. No hot and cold running water or refrigeration as we know them today. No washers, dryers, television sets, or radios.

Consider the Prevailing Forms of Leadership Leaders were tribal elders for the early parts of the Old Testament, then judges and priests, then kings (and very often, prophets who opposed them). Egyptian pharaohs and slavery. Babylonian exile. Roman occupation. The Middle East has always been a land in political and military turmoil.

Consider the Family Relationships There were often close loyal ties, but mobility was highly limited within a family or tribe. Positions of status were fixed, with siblings often postured as rivals as they sought to gain family power and influence.

Consider the Religious and Societal Norms
Pharisees and Sadducees claimed spiritual superiority. The masses were burdened by guilt and sin but were unable to "keep the law" as they perceived it.

How can you learn about the historical context?

1. Consult a Bible dictionary or encyclopedia. Look up the names of people, places, customs, and things.

2. Read books about Bible times.

3. Read historically accurate novels set in Bible times.

4. Peruse archaeological books and magazines, especially *Biblical Archaeology Review.*

The more you know about the ways in which the people of the Bible lived, the more vivid the Bible's stories and teachings will be to you—and the more meaning you will glean from the Scriptures.

31 ■ How Can I Use This Information Today?

The Bible will seem much more relevant to you if you make three assumptions at the outset of your reading of any passage:

1. This Has Something to Do with Me or God Wouldn't Have Put It in the Bible Every part of the Bible is for every person. Assume that every passage you read has been written exclusively for you, as if it is a private letter directly from heaven to your doorstep. Ask yourself frequently, What am I supposed to learn from this?

2. I Can Use This Information in Some Way The Bible's teachings aren't only for your information. They are for your application. You are expected to use what you learn. Jesus taught, "Not everyone who says to Me, 'Lord, Lord,' shall enter the kingdom of heaven, but he who does the will of My Father in heaven" (Matt. 7:21). James 1:22 reiterates this teaching: "Be doers of the word, and not hearers only, deceiving yourselves."

3. It's Important for Me to Know This Information Because It Has Eternal Consequences

The Bible doesn't deal with passing fads. It presents eternal truth. Part of that eternal truth is the eventual judgment of God at the crossroads between time and eternity. The standard by which we will be judged, through the grace of Jesus, is the Bible.

Scriptural Signposts   Frequently as you read the Bible, one or more verses will seem to leap out at you—as a promise, as a point of conviction (about something you need to change in your life), or as a reassurance. That's God's way of shining a spotlight on the piece of information you need in this hour, this day, this month so that you may grow, endure, or have the courage to act. Take a moment to write down that verse and post it somewhere. Let it nurture you.

If a small plaque, notecard, or picture speaks to you in a special way, put it where you'll see it often. Small promise cards can be purchased with inspirational Scriptures; consider carrying a new one in your wallet each day where you will see it whenever you make a purchase or are asked to provide identification. Draw strength from the Word. Let it mold your behavior, your attitude, and your aspirations.

Don't keep the Word of God at arm's length. Internalize it. Let it feed you, encourage you, and change you!

EXPLORING THE BREADTH AND DEPTH OF THE BIBLE'S MEANING

32. Consider a Yearly Read-Through Plan

You may choose from a number of one-year reading plans and methods. Some are included as part of daily devotional guides; a plan is generally included in a Bible with "helps"; still others are available in bookmark form at your local Bible bookstore.

Most plans call for you to read a portion of the Old Testament and a portion of the New Testament every day—perhaps one reading in the morning and another in the evening. Sometimes an additional passage from Psalms or Proverbs is recommended.

Still others suggest reading four pages a day—choosing one book at a time, at your discretion, and completing an entire book before moving on to the next.

The good news is that all of these plans work! Choose the one you think you will enjoy the most.

A One-Year Bible   One young woman worked with a One-Year Bible. The Bible had already been segmented into 365 readings, each several pages long. Although she was not a disciplined reader, she began reading on January 1 and finished the last words of Revelation on December 31.

A Self-Made Plan   On the other hand, one young man limited himself to a goal of reading only the New Testament in a year. The New Testament in his Bible had 348 pages, so he set a goal of reading at least one page a day. However, some days, he became so involved in what he was reading that he read a few extra pages. He finished the New Testament in July and decided to "sample" the Old Testament, reading a book at a time as he desired. To his surprise, by the end of the year he had read more than half the Old Testament, too.

A Schedule   The two key advantages of a one-year reading schedule are these:

1. *Personal discipline in reading the Bible.* A prescribed schedule or method helps you develop the habit of daily Bible reading.

2. *Better understanding of the whole.* By reading the entire Bible in a relatively short period of time, you'll be able to see specific passages more clearly in the context of the entire Bible, and you'll become more adept at seeing Genesis-to-Revelation themes, repeated symbols, and the hallmarks of God's master plan for humankind's redemption and salvation.

33. Read an Entire Book

Many books in the Bible are short enough to read in one sitting—thirty minutes or less.

Ecclesiastes   This book of wisdom was written by King Solomon who set his heart to "search out by wisdom concerning all that is done under heaven" (1:13).

Esther   The beautiful Hebrew girl became queen in a foreign land and courageously saved her people from destruction.

Jonah   God called a man to preach righteousness to an otherwise doomed city.

Ruth   A faithful daughter-in-law was rewarded richly for her obedience to God's call upon her life.

James   Five powerful chapters tell us how faith works.

Jude   This one will fit in a ten-minute reading session. The twenty-five verses are packed with wisdom about the need to contend for the faith against false teachers and heresies.

1, 2, and 3 John   Three powerful letters portray a life committed to loving God and loving others.

1 and 2 Peter   These letters to persons living under persecution cover topics related to Christian behavior.

The Letters of Paul   Galatians, Ephesians, Philippians, and Colossians are six chapters or less in length. These books can't be digested in a sitting, but you'll get a good feel for the whole of each one by reading it through in its entirety, which is the way that the believers in each of these churches first heard them.

Old Testament Prophets   The prophetic utterances of Joel, Nahum, Habakkuk, Zephaniah, Haggai, and Malachi are short enough to be read in one sitting.

Obadiah   You will find the prophecy in these twenty-one verses as current as today's newspaper. Verse 4 proclaims,

"Though you ascend as high as the eagle,
And though you set your nest among the stars,
From there I will bring you down," says the LORD.

34 · A Daily Helping of Psalms and Proverbs

When a skeptical lawyer tried to trick Jesus by asking Him, "Which is the great commandment in the law?" Jesus replied,

> "You shall love the LORD your God with all your heart, with all your soul, and with all your mind." This is the first and great commandment. And the second is like it: "You shall love your neighbor as yourself." On these two commandments hang all the Law and the Prophets (Matt. 22:35–40).

It has been said that the book of Psalms describes the relationship of humanity to God and the book of Proverbs describes the relationship of humanity to humanity. Reading a portion of the Psalms and a portion of the book of Proverbs every day keeps our hearts continually turned toward fulfilling the Lord's words: loving God, and loving others as ourselves.

Psalms   Nearly every emotion known to humankind can be found in this collection of 150 "songs." Sorrow, anger, hurt, loneliness, despair—

all are there. Love, faith, hope, joy, high praise, and worship—you'll find them in the Psalms! You'll even discover an antidote for sleep and a passage about swimming in your tears (Pss. 4:8; 6:6).

If you read an average of five psalms a day—or about three pages—you'll finish the entire book in a month and have the satisfaction of having completed the longest book in the Bible.

You can use the Psalms as a basis for prayer, too. Personalize them whenever you can. You can also sing the Psalms. Make up your own tunes.

Proverbs   The book of Proverbs is perhaps the most directly practical of all books in the Bible. Try reading one chapter a day for a month to finish the thirty-one chapters. By reading just a few verses a day, you can finish the book in a year.

You'll find practical words of wisdom such as:

Better is a dry morsel with quietness, than a house full of feasting with strife (Prov. 17:1).

Whoever is a partner with a thief hates his own life (Prov. 29:24).

Hope deferred makes the heart sick (Prov. 13:12).

The books of Psalms and Proverbs are excellent ones to commit to memory over time. Meditate on a verse daily. Rehearse it frequently. Make it a part of the way you live.

35. Read the Words of Jesus

Read the words of Jesus as you come to them in sequence. Most are found in the four Gospels. Several passages are in the Acts of the Apostles, the Epistles, and Revelation.

Some Bibles print the words of Jesus in red. Read a few of the black-letter words or sentences before each red-letter passage to gain the context of His truths. Consider that Jesus is speaking directly to you as you read.

After you are familiar with the words of Jesus (perhaps as the result of a one-time overview reading), go back and study His words. You can do this in several different ways.

Read All of the Gospel Cross-References
These references are often provided in a Bible (in margins or as notes for each verse in the text). Note the differences and similarities, and which passages are duplicated. Duplicated passages are likely the most prominent messages that Jesus preached.

The Scriptures teach that by two witnesses the truth is established. If the Bible states something even once it is important; the second witness will be the Holy Spirit as He quickens the passage to your heart. If a commandment or teaching is written twice or more, it should be considered of utmost importance.

Read All of the Old Testament Cross-References   You'll probably be surprised at how much Jesus quoted the Old Testament in His teaching.

Read the Other New Testament Cross-References   Notice how often the apostles quoted Jesus as they instructed their first Christian converts.

The apostles lived by Jesus' words, as all who trust Him as Savior are asked to do. Jesus said to His followers, "Behold, I give you the authority to trample on serpents and scorpions, and over all the power of the enemy, and nothing shall by any means hurt you" (Luke 10:19). Paul trusted this promise when a poisonous snake came out of a campfire he was helping to build and fastened onto his hand. He shook the viper back into the fire and was not harmed. (See Acts 28:5.)

Read the Words of Jesus in Composite Sequence   Some Bibles have a "helps" section that outlines Jesus' ministry in sequence, blending together the four Gospels.

Reread Portions Related to the Kingdom of God   Jesus taught a great deal about the kingdom of God and the kingdom of heaven. Study His parables and teachings about them.

36 ∎ Choose-a-Word Studies

Do a word study. Choose a word, preferably a noun, of your interest. It may be *fish* or *cup* or *time*. And then consult a concordance. A concordance lists Scripture references under a topical word along with a few descriptive words from the verse cited.

Your Bible may have an abbreviated concordance. Or you may want to invest in a Bible concordance. You can purchase a paperback version of *Cruden's Complete Concordance*—a good, basic concordance, handy in size and not too detailed—for just a few dollars at your favorite Bible bookstore. *Young's* and *Strong's* are larger, more complete concordances to consider.

Procedure Have paper and pencil handy and then:

Look up the word in an alphabetically arranged concordance.

List the references next to it, leaving ample space to make notes. In some cases, the list may be quite long, with references spanning from Genesis to Revelation. Choose a few references from both Old and New Testaments.

Look up each reference. Read a few verses before

and after the one cited. After you've read, write a few words about what that verse means to you.

You may want to take several days to complete your study for a word that has many references. Keep your choose-a-word studies in a notebook so you can refer to them easily in the future—possibly to expand them, teach from them, consult them in times of difficulty, or review them for your own instruction. Word studies make excellent devotional lessons.

One of the foremost benefits of word studies is that they are always fresh and relevant because the words are of your own choosing.

A Sample Word Study: Money

Nearly everybody has an interest in money. Here are eight references and a question next to each to trigger your own comments:

1. *Genesis 23:9*—What qualities does God expect me to exhibit in my business transactions?

2. *Exodus 21:11*—What should be my motivation for giving?

3. *Deuteronomy 23:19–20*—Is it right to charge interest on loans I make to family members or fellow Christians?

4. *Luke 19:12–27*—Does the Bible advocate a profit motive?

5. *Acts 8:18*—What about people who attempt to buy their way into God's favor?

6. *1 Timothy 6:10*—What really is the root of all evil? (Hint: it isn't money in and of itself.)

37 ▪ Journey Studies

The Bible is filled with journeys. In our highly mobile society, with people continually on the move, we usually find it easy to relate to journeys and to comprehend their meaning.

Your Journey As you read about a journey, compare it to your own experience on life's road. Look for

- the goal of the journey. Where are the persons going? Why? Are they just traveling, or are they planning to arrive at a specific destination? Is it a forced or runaway move?
- the detours. Nearly every journey involves side trips. Are the detours chosen or forced? Are they the result of obedience, rebellion, an escape from famine, a search for fortune?
- the means of guidance. What are the signposts? Does God use stunning signs and wonders to lead people, or does He rely on them to obey His previous commandments?
- hallmarks of the journey. What happens during the journey? How is the person changed on the outside and on the inside?

A Sample Journey: Joseph   One of the Bible's most meaningful journeys is that of Joseph (Gen. 37—50). You'll find several subtopics to explore: sibling rivalry, the dynamics of a large nomadic family, rejection, slavery, imprisonment, sexual temptation, the interpretation of dreams, political savvy, the pressures and privileges of power.

God's guidance is evident in every stage of the journey, but Joseph's obedience to the Lord doesn't necessarily keep him from danger, misunderstandings, loneliness, or rejection. At the same time, Joseph's steadfastness keeps him in a position to receive God's great blessings and to save his family from starvation.

As you read Joseph's story, ask yourself,

• How did he feel when this happened?
• Why did he act as he did or say what he said?
• What character traits are developing in him through this experience?
• How is my life's journey like that of Joseph?

Other Journey Studies   Some other noteworthy journeys are those of these individuals:

• Jonah—see the book of Jonah
• Ruth and Naomi—see the book of Ruth
• David—see 1 Samuel
• Paul—see Acts 7; 13—28

38 ▪ Biblical Heroes and Heroines

Biographies and autobiographies remain two of the most popular book genres on the market today —as they have been since the early days of publishing. We simply like to read about other human beings. And that is certainly true of the life stories of people we have come to know as biblical heroes and heroines.

Suggested Questions   As you read the story of a major figure, ask yourself,

- What was the world like when the person was alive? What were the physical conditions of the environment? What was the cultural and political climate of the time?
- Into what circumstances was the person born? And how did those circumstances change?
- What happened that was beyond personal control? What happened as a result of deliberate decisions?
- What special traits or talents did the person possess?
- What was the reward for the person's sheer

obedience and endurance of faith? How long
was it before the results came?

• What was the person's relationship with God?
How did that relationship begin? How did it
develop?

Of course, you don't need to limit yourself to the
people we regard as influential leaders of biblical
times. Explore lesser-known characters the Creator trusted.

Suggested Heroes and Heroines for Study

Abigail	Jesus	Paul
Abraham	John	Peter
Daniel	Jonathan	Priscilla
David	Joshua	Rebecca
Deborah	Mary and	Ruth
Elijah	Martha	Samuel
Elisha	Mary, mother	Sarah
Esther	of Jesus	Shunammite
Gideon	Miriam	woman
Hannah	Moses	Solomon
Jacob	Noah	Timothy

By studying some Bible villains and those who
may have started out close to God and then rebelled or disobeyed, we can learn about what not
to do.

Adam and Eve   Jacob and   Pharaoh
Ahab and   Esau   Samson and
  Jezebel   Jonah   Delilah
Cain   Judas   Saul

A Sample Study   Turn to the book of
Job. In addition to the questions at the beginning
of this chapter, ask yourself, How would I have
responded had I been Job? Which of Job's friends
would I have been most like? What does this book
say to me about suffering? Have I ever acted as
Job's wife did? What set Job apart from other men
in God's eyes? What caused Job's circumstances to
change? What did God require of Job?

39 ▪ Current Issue Studies

No matter what the issue capturing our attention (through news magazines and newspapers, on television news and talk shows), the Bible has something to say about it.

What Does the Bible Say? As you encounter key issues that compel you to take a stand or forge an opinion, ask yourself, I wonder what the Bible says?

At times, your search through the Scriptures may resemble a word study (Chapter 36) or a subject study (Chapter 41). At times, you may find most of the answers you want through using a Bible cyclopedic index, which is arranged more topically than a concordance. In many cases, you'll find references that give examples of the issue as well as teachings about it.

You may find a topical Bible (such as *Nave's*) to be of help in discovering what the Bible says about current issues. In a topical Bible, the key references about a topic or issue are written out in their entirety and then additional references are provided.

Suggested Current Issue Studies   See what the Bible has to say about some of these issues in our society today:

- Marriage, husband, wife, children, abortion, divorce
- Race, prejudice, class distinction, slavery
- Adultery, fornication, incest, homosexuality
- Debt, cheating, stealing
- Work, employment, poverty
- Wine, drunkenness, alcoholism, drug dependency
- Devil, demon possession, idols, occultism
- Disease
- Death, murder, capital punishment
- Freedom, war
- Trade, commerce
- Earthquake, flood, fire, drought
- Energy, earth, environment, conservation, pollution
- Education, edification, preparation

In a broader sense, you may want to look up *sin* and *abomination* to gain a sense of what God truly considers to be the right and wrong ways for us to live in relationship with one another.

40 ▪ Prayers in the Bible

Frequent topics in the Bible are prayer—communication with God—and people who pray faithfully. The Bible calls us to be people of prayer. God desires for His people to talk to Him—to request things of Him, to thank Him, to praise Him, to rely upon Him, to worship Him.

Prayer, in its simplest form, is talking to God. It's expressing your thoughts and feelings to your Creator, who loves you and is eager to listen to you. It's repenting, asking for forgiveness of sins. It's praising God for His creation of you, His preservation of your life, and the blessings He has given you. It's worshiping God for who He is, the Lord almighty. Anytime you find someone in the Scriptures talking to God—however short or long the statement, regardless of surroundings—you can consider that to be prayer.

By studying the prayers, you'll discover God's answers to those prayers. You'll uncover some of the most intimate, heartfelt moments in the Bible.

Prayers to Study   Here are some of the foremost prayers you may want to study:

- Moses' Praise   Exod. 15:1–18
- Hezekiah's Prayer   2 Kings 20:3

- The Lord's Prayer   Matt. 6:9–13
  (our model for
  daily prayer)
- Hannah's Prayer   1 Sam. 1:10–18
- Mary's Prayer   Luke 1:46–55
- Jehoshaphat's   2 Chron. 20:5–12
  Prayer
- Peter's Prayer   Acts 4:23–31
- Stephen's Prayer   Acts 7:59–60
- Jesus' Prayer for   John 17:1–5
  Himself
- Jesus' Prayer for   John 17:6–19
  Apostles
- Jesus' Prayer for   John 17:20–26
  Us
- Jesus' Prayer in   Matt. 26:36–46
  Gethsemane
- Paul's Prayer for   Phil. 1:1–11
  Philippians

Prayers in the Gospels and Acts   Jesus seems repeatedly to have been on His way to a place of prayer, in a place of prayer, or coming from a place of prayer. The same is true for the apostles as they spread the good news.

As you read about biblical men and women of prayer, ask yourself,

- What is their attitude of heart and mind?
- What are the characteristics of the prayer? Are they alone or with others? Are they petitioning or praising? Are they interceding for

others or praying for themselves? Are they confessing sin? Are they in high worship? Is the person in a position with head bowed, eyes closed, and hands folded or in another position?
- What is being requested or said?
- What circumstance is compelling the person to pray?
- How does God respond?

Reading the answered prayers of the Bible builds faith—for us to request things of God, with faith, and to look for the solution to needs in our lives.

41 ■ Subject Studies

A good question to trigger a subject study is this: I wonder what God thinks about . . . ? Oftentimes, you can begin a subject study by asking this question about a passage you are reading as part of your ten-minute-a-day discipline. The goal of a subject study is to discover biblical truths about a subject.

Begin your subject study by

- making notes about what you already know or believe about the topic. Ask the Holy Spirit to bring related verses or teachings you have heard in the past to your remembrance.
- writing down questions about the topic.

Contemplation   Contemplation—which requires both relaxed time and a peaceful environment—is the wandering of your mind and spirit under the inspiration of the Holy Spirit. It begins with a sincere prayer:

Holy Spirit, guide me into Your truth about this matter.

The process of contemplation is often triggered by questions such as these:

- What are synonyms for or words related to the central topic under study? For example, in our previous example of money, some related words might be: *stealing, leasing, borrowing, give/giving, lending, investing, wealth, riches, greed, rich, poor, stingy, generous, poverty, possessions, bribes,* and so forth. Consider related adjectives (such as *abundant*) and words related to function (such as *buy*).
- What are some opposites or antonyms? For example, in dealing with money some words might be *lack* and *poverty.*
- What are some ingredients necessary to make an object or from which a situation is created? Again, in relationship to money, some examples might be silver, gold, wages, inheritance.
- What are emotions often related to the subject? With regard to money, one might feel fear (at not having enough), loss (at time of bankruptcy), or blessing (at a sudden increase).

Look up the related words in your concordance, and then follow through on the references.

As you undertake this study, you'll discover that you have a clearer understanding about God's unchanging opinion on a topic. You'll gain independence in studying the Bible. And you'll grow rapidly in your overall understanding of God's Word.

A Sample Subject Study: Children
Since each of us has been a child, we all can relate!

Ask: What does it mean to be a child? What are attributes of children? What is important to children? Why did Jesus admonish us to become as little children?

Make lists and notes. Explore the characteristics of children and the aspects common to their behavior. Consider the concepts of play, trust, dependency, curiosity, learning, growth, and security.

Ask: What are the characteristics of adulthood as opposed to childhood? What are the marks of maturity? How does a child learn and grow into adulthood? What is my responsibility as a parent, godparent, or other adult relative to the children in my life? What is my responsibility as an adult to all those who are younger than I am in the faith? Consider closely related words: *mother, father, son, daughter.*

Ask: How can I recognize and nurture these qualities in children: esteem, anticipation, affection, joy, and love? How can I help a child who feels frustration, fear, or sorrow?

Contemplate the functions of helping children—caregiving, sharing, punishment, discipline, reward, training, giving of time, talents, and energy.

42 ■ Follow the Chain

Bible verses can often be strung together—one relating to the next and the next and the next. The process of constructing a Bible chain is a little like the tale of the man who found the end of a rope and followed it and followed it all the way to the treasure chest. Scripture chains are especially easy to construct if your Bible provides references in a center margin or as verse endnotes.

A Sample Chain Romans 6:23 says, "For the wages of sin is death, but the gift of God is eternal life in Christ Jesus our Lord." Two references are provided in one Bible: Genesis 2:17 and 1 Peter 1:4.

Genesis 2:17 takes you back to the Garden of Eden and God's command in teaching Adam and Eve obedience—that they will die if they eat of the fruit from the forbidden tree. References provided there point to Genesis 3:14–19, the curses put on the serpent, woman, man, and earth. One reference provided is Romans 16:19–20, which leads to Romans 1:8. Another reference is Deuteronomy 28:15–20, which provides references to Leviticus 26:24–39; Malachi 2:2; Isaiah 65:14; and Isaiah 30:17.

By now, you may be nearly overwhelmed by the idea of the punishment of the Lord for disobedience. Read beyond Leviticus 26:39 to move into the promises of restoration. There, you find references to Psalm 136:23–26; Psalm 98:2; and Romans 11:28. Following the Psalm 136 reference, you are led to Genesis 8:1; Psalm 44:7; and Psalm 104:27, where you experience God's mercy and personal care.

Following the Psalm 98:2 reference, you come to Luke 3:6, which leads you to Isaiah 40:5, which takes you to Isaiah 35:2, which compels you to read Isaiah 32:15, and from there, Isaiah 29:17 and Joel 2:28. In following the reference in Joel, you are led to Ezekiel 39:29; Zechariah 12:10; Isaiah 54:13; Acts 21:9; and Galatians 3:28. You bask in the peace of His promises for your family; you are confronted with your responsibilities as a priest in your home; and you are reminded of the events associated with the end times. What a tremendous, earth-encompassing, Holy-Spirit-given blessing is available to those who will obey the Lord and accept the sacrifice of God's Son for our sins!

Going back to the beginning, follow 1 Peter 1:4 to Colossians 1:3–5, which takes you to Philippians 1:3–7.

In all, you have chained together some thirty verses and gained bold insight into the two fates held before each one of us: a life of obedience and acceptance of God's commandments and sacrifice, which leads to an overwhelming blessing, or a life of rebellion and rejection of God, which leads to devastation and destruction.

43 ▪ Miracles of the Bible

A study of the miracles of the Bible will no doubt lead you to this overwhelming conclusion: God can do anything!

The more you read the miracles in both Old and New Testaments, the more your spirit will explode into faith to believe God for what you need.

Here are a few of God's miracles:

Forgiveness of Sins
- Paralytic   Mark 2:3–12
- Malefactor on cross   Luke 23:32–34
  at Crucifixion

Deliverance from Enemies
- Syrian army put to   2 Kings 7:6–7
  flight
- Sennacherib's army   2 Kings 19:35
  destroyed

Healing and Restoration
- Naaman healed of   2 Kings 5:10–14
  leprosy
- Snake-bitten   Num. 21:7–9
  Israelites healed
- Leper healed   Mark 1:40–45

- Jairus's daughter   Mark 5:22–43
  raised to life
- Woman with issue   Mark 5:25–34
  of blood healed
- Blind Bartimaeus's   Mark 10:46–52
  eyes restored

Provision
- Water into wine   John 2:1–11
- Feeding of 5,000   Mark 6:35–44
- Miracle catch of   Luke 5:1–11
  fish
- Widow's oil and   1 Kings 17:10–16
  meal supplied
- Waters of Marah   Exod. 15:23–25
  made sweet
- Manna and quail   Exod. 16:13–35
  provided

Protection
- Three Hebrew men   Dan. 3:19–27
  in furnace
- Daniel in lions' den Dan. 6:16–23

Deliverance from Demon Power
- Gadarene demoniac   Mark 5:1–20
- Blind and mute   Matt. 12:22–23
  demoniac
- Son with demonic   Mark 9:14–39
  seizures

Power Over the Elements of Nature
- Sun standing still   Josh. 10:13
- Jesus stilling a   Mark 4:39
  storm
- Red Sea parted   Exod. 14:21
- Elijah stopping the   2 Kings 2:8
  Jordan
- Jesus walks on   Mark 6:45–52
  water

Omnipotence   Bear in mind as you study the miracles of the Bible that God is omnipotent—all-powerful. He has all the resources of the universe at His command. He can literally move heaven and earth on your behalf.

Omniscience   God is omniscient—all-knowing and all-wise. He sees the ending from the beginning. He will not act on your behalf to the detriment of another person; He will not countermand His own laws and principles.

Omnipresence   God is omnipresent. He governs time and timing. His answers and provisions for you are always given within the context of eternity.

Love   Finally, God is loving. He will do nothing to lead to your harm or destruction; He desires only what will bless you and train you toward perfection in Christ Jesus.

44 ▪ An Isaiah Study

The book of Isaiah has sixty-six chapters, the same number as the total number of books in the Bible (Old and New Testaments). The amazing thing is that each chapter seems to correspond with a book.

How to Proceed In exploring this correlation, write in pencil the names of the books of the Bible alongside the chapter numbers of Isaiah. For example, next to chapter 1, write Genesis, next to chapter 11, write 1 Kings, and so forth. Then take a couple of months in your ten-minute-a-day reading discipline and do the following:

1. Read a chapter of Isaiah each day.

2. Go to the book of the Bible corresponding to the chapter and read through all of the subheads provided. Skim through the contents of the book; recall what you know about the material. Review any notes in the text or margins.

3. Draw a conclusion. What seems to be one, or a few, of the themes central to both the chapter in Isaiah and the book?

For example, the first chapter of Isaiah can be correlated to the book of Genesis. Key words and phrases in the chapter will trigger thoughts of creation, Adam and Eve, Cain and Abel, Abraham and Sarah, Isaac, Jacob, and Joseph, such as:

- "The LORD has spoken: 'I have nourished and brought up children, and they have rebelled against Me'" (v. 2). How does this relate to Adam and Eve, the Tower of Babel, Noah, the citizens of Sodom, and Jacob?
- "Unless the LORD of hosts had left to us a very small remnant, we would have become like Sodom, we would have been made like Gomorrah" (v. 9). How does this relate to Genesis 19?

The second chapter of Isaiah evokes remembrances of the book of Exodus. You'll find references such as:

- "Enter into the rock, and hide in the dust, from the terror of the LORD and the glory of His majesty" (v. 10). Recall how the children of Israel felt as Moses went up into the mountain to meet with the Lord.

What You Learn   A study of Isaiah—and a corresponding review of the other books of the Bible—will help you to see repeated themes throughout the Bible. It is an excellent way to review the Bible's contents.

45 ▪ Heaven

The Bible promises that ultimately, one day, those of us who believe in the Lord Jesus and have accepted His death on the cross as our personal redemption from the consequences of sin will live forever with our heavenly Father. That is the promise of Jesus in the Bible verse quoted more often than all others, John 3:16: "For God so loved the world that He gave His only begotten Son, that whoever believes in Him should not perish but have everlasting life."

Jesus also said,

Let not your heart be troubled; you believe in God, believe also in Me. In My Father's house are many mansions; if it were not so, I would have told you. I go to prepare a place for you. And if I go and prepare a place for you, I will come again and receive you to Myself; that where I am, there you may be also (John 14:1–3).

Glimpses of Eternity The Bible is not only a handbook for the earth; it also lifts us from our temporary bounds by giving us glimpses of our lives in eternity. When the problems of this earth seem especially complex and the burdens exceedingly heavy, do a study on heaven. Our destiny is to be with Jesus in heaven forever. What a great future to anticipate!

Perhaps the most descriptive passage in the Bible about heaven is in Revelation 21—22, the last two chapters of the Bible. Read them aloud. Elsewhere, you'll find references that add to this description.

The Bible Tells Us Who Is in Heaven See 1 Kings 8:30; Psalm 139:7–8; Matthew 19:14; Hebrews 9:12, 24; 12:22–23. You'll want to be with them.

The Bible Tells Us What Is Absent from Heaven See Luke 20:36; 1 Corinthians 15:50; Revelation 7:17; 21:4; 22:4–5, 15. You'll be glad to do without these things.

The Bible Tells Us What Heaven Will Be Like See Matthew 5:11–12; Luke 15:7, 10; 16:19–25; Romans 8:17–18; 1 Peter 1:4; 2 Peter 3:13; Revelation 7:15; 14:13. You'll be ecstatic upon arrival.

The Bible Tells Us How to Get into Heaven See Matthew 5:20; John 3:5, 18, 21; 1 Corinthians 15:51; 1 Peter 1:10–11; Revelation 2:7, 10–11; 19:8; 22:14. You'll be glad you know God's Word and have applied it to your life.

A study of heaven purifies us. When heaven is in the forefront of our thinking, we don't want to do anything that will detract from our heavenly reward or our future in the presence of the most holy God.

46 ▪ Discover the Messiah

The Old Testament speaks repeatedly of Messiah —"the promised anointed One" of God who will one day come to deliver His people forever from evil and wickedness.

The New Testament proclaims that Messiah has come—that Jesus Christ is Messiah, our Savior and Lord forever!

	Prophecy	Fulfilled
• Seed of a woman	Gen. 3:15	Gal. 4:4
• Abraham's descendant	Gen. 12:3	Matt. 1:1
• Isaac's descendant	Gen. 17:19	Luke 3:34
• Jacob's descendant	Num. 24:17	Matt. 1:2
• From tribe of Judah	Gen. 49:10	Luke 3:33
• Heir to David's throne	Isa. 9:7	Luke 1:32

• Born in Bethlehem	Mic. 5:2	Luke 2:4, 5, 7
• Born of a virgin	Isa. 7:14	Luke 1:26–27, 30–31
• Spared from early murder	Jer. 31:15	Matt. 2:16–18
• Flight to Egypt	Hos. 11:1	Matt. 2:14–15
• A prophet forerunner	Isa. 40:3–5 Mal. 3:1 Mal. 4:5–6	Luke 3:3–6 Luke 7:24, 27 Matt. 11:13–14
• Called the Son of God	Ps. 2:7	Matt. 3:17
• Ministry in Galilee	Isa. 9:1–2	Matt. 4:13–16
• Parable teacher	Ps. 78:2–4	Matt. 13:34–35
• A prophet	Deut. 18:15	Acts 3:20, 22
• Binder of broken-hearted	Isa. 61:1–2	Luke 4:18–19
• Rejected by Jewish rulers	Isa. 53:3	John 1:11
• Priest like Melchizedek	Ps. 110:4	Hebr. 5:5–6
• Triumphant entry	Zech. 9:9	Mark 11:7, 9, 11
• Adored by infants	Ps. 8:2	Matt. 21:15–16
• Not believed	Isa. 53:1	John 12:37–38

• Betrayed by friend for money	Ps. 41:9 Zech. 11:12	Luke 22:47–48 Matt. 26:14–15
• Accused falsely	Ps. 35:11	Mark 14:57–58
• Silent when accused	Isa. 53:7	Mark 15:4–5
• Spat upon and struck	Isa. 50:6	Matt. 27:30
• Hated without reason	Ps. 35:19	John 15:24
• Sacrifice in our place	Isa. 53:5	Rom. 5:6, 8
• Crucified with criminals	Isa. 53:12	Mark 15:27–28
• Hands and feet pierced	Zech. 12:10	John 20:27
• Mocked and reproached	Ps. 22:7–8 Ps. 69:9	Luke 23:35 Rom. 15:3
• Prays for enemies	Ps. 109:4	Luke 23:34
• Soldiers gamble for clothes	Ps. 22:17–18	Matt. 27:35–36
• Forsaken by Father God	Ps. 22:1	Matt. 27:46
• No bones broken	Ps. 34:20	John 19:32–33, 36
• Side pierced	Zech. 12:10	John 19:34

• Buried among rich	Isa. 53:9	Matt. 27:57–60
• Resurrected from dead	Ps. 16:10 Ps. 49:15	Mark 16:6–7
• Ascended to Father's right hand	Ps. 68:18	Mark 16:19 1 Cor. 15:4 Eph. 4:8

47 ■ Progression Studies

Our spiritual life in Christ is expected to grow. As the apostle Paul wrote, we are to "grow up in all things into Him who is the head—Christ" (Eph. 4:15). The apostle Peter stated it this way: we are to "grow in the grace and knowledge of our Lord and Savior Jesus Christ" (2 Pet. 3:18).

Numerous passages in the Bible present growth concepts in a stepping-stone manner. One concept builds upon a previous one—as if taking another step up the ladder to spiritual maturity.

Matthew 5:3–10   The beatitudes can be studied as a progression.

Matthew 5:3 When we recognize we are "poor in spirit," we know that our spirit is inadequate, incomplete, and empty. We have a need that only the Almighty can meet. He does that through Jesus' sacrifice by sending His comforting Spirit to infuse our poor spirit. And through this salvation, He gives us the kingdom of heaven.

Matthew 5:4 The next step is mourning for our loved ones we know are not ready to meet God. He has promised to save not only us but our entire household. We are comforted as we witness to them by the leading of the Holy Spirit (Acts 16:31).

Matthew 5:5 To be "meek" means to desire to be under the authority of the Lord. Those who subject themselves to God's authority can be trusted with positions of service on the earth.

Matthew 5:6 Next, as we hunger and thirst for more of God's righteousness on the earth, we find that our righteousness is established. We personally seek the refreshing of the Holy Spirit for our thirsty souls. The ever-available Spirit of truth brings revelation of the Scriptures to satisfy our hunger with meat of the Word, instead of milk (1 Cor. 2:12).

There are more steps in this progression, but this example shows how one concept leads to the next.

Psalms 22, 23, and 24

Note the Messiah's sacrifice and agony for our sins. The believers accept the Lord as Savior and Shepherd, see the Lord as provider in every area of life, regard the Lord as protector in all circumstances, accept a royal appointment in God's kingdom, anticipate an eternal dwellingplace in heaven.

Galatians 5:22–23

One characteristic gives rise to the next as we bear the fruit of the Spirit.

Ephesians 3:14–19

Persons pray with boldness and confidence in their access to God. Look especially for a progression in what God gives to those who pray.

1 Thessalonians 5:16–18   Believers unite to form a strong spiritual network in anticipation of the Lord's return.

As you undertake a progression study, follow these recommendations:

Read the Whole   Then dissect the parts.

Look for a Strong Relationship Among the Verses   Be wary of contriving a relationship that doesn't exist.

Check Your Progression Against Other Scriptures   If your interpretation isn't supported by other passages in the Bible, you're on the wrong track.

Check to See If the Last Verse or Part of the Passage Leads to a Closer Relationship with the Lord Jesus than the First   Progressions always lead upward! They point toward growth in our understanding and in our relationship with Jesus.

48 ▪ Type-and-Shadow Studies

In studying the Old Testament, look for the people, objects, and events that cast spiritual shadows. The writer of the book of Hebrews indicated that much in the Old Testament served as a "copy and shadow of the heavenly things" (Heb. 8:5). In his letter to the Colossian church, the apostle Paul noted that many customs and events of the Old Testament were a "shadow of things to come, but the substance is of Christ" (Col. 2:17).

In a type-and-shadow study we take a physical, natural, material person, place, event, thing, or journey as a spiritual prototype. We view it in light of the coming of Christ and the Holy Spirit, the development of the church, and the growth of an individual believer.

A Sample Study   The book of Ruth may be studied as a type and shadow of the way in which the Holy Spirit leads us to Jesus. In this drama, let Naomi represent the Holy Spirit. We are like Ruth. Boaz represents Jesus.

In the beginning of the story, Ruth faces a decision. Will she follow Naomi or return to her previous life? The Holy Spirit confronts us with that same decision: Will we move forward with Him or turn back to our sin?

As Ruth travels with Naomi toward her homeland in Bethlehem, they face no enemies and no temptations, but they are separated from others. Very often we find ourselves feeling alone and detached as we follow the leading of the Holy Spirit away from our sinful colleagues and toward Christ Jesus.

The kinsman of Naomi is Boaz. The Holy Spirit also has a kinsman: Jesus! He has a field of grain that is the Word of God. Naomi sends Ruth into the fields to work for Boaz; she admonishes Ruth to work only for Boaz. The Holy Spirit leads us to the Word of God and says, "Glean here." The day comes when He begins to feed us with spiritual insights and revelations, just as Boaz served food to Ruth.

As the story concludes, Ruth has developed an intimate, loving, personal, nurturing, fulfilling relationship with Boaz. The Holy Spirit leads us to the same type of relationship with Jesus. We come to His feet in perfect submission, and He redeems us and calls us His own.

Other Studies   These additional books make excellent type-and-shadow studies: Esther; Exodus; Job; Jonah; Joshua; and Song of Solomon.

Many Old Testament stories can be personally applied by types and shadows to give you more understanding in your spiritual pilgrimage. Look for them.

49 ▪ Symbol Studies

Symbols occur in every book of the Bible, and in many cases, our ability to understand a symbol unlocks the meaning of an entire story or teaching. Symbols indicate eternal values, means, and reasons.

Numbers are often used as symbols in the Bible —especially the numbers six (for humankind), seven (for the fullness of God), eight (for perfection and new beginning), and ten (for increase).

Colors are often symbols, such as *white* for purification and holiness; *red* for blood and redemption; *black* for sin; and *gold* for God's glory.

Tangible objects—such as oil (indicative of the Holy Spirit) and water (cleansing or baptism)— may also be studied as symbols.

A symbol must carry the same meaning in every reference in the Bible for the symbolic meaning to be valid. The symbol must have a consistent meaning that holds up in all references. If you question the meaning or interpretation of a symbol, check Bible commentaries and reference books to see what the scholars say.

Suggested Studies   Many Bible passages lend themselves to symbol study:

- *Noah's ark* (Gen. 6)
  Hint: the ark had three stories—animals on the lower deck, people on the middle deck, and a window toward heaven. View the ark as a person—body, soul, and spirit.
- *Nehemiah's wall* (Neh. 2—3)
  Hint: the wall is the invisible presence of the Holy Spirit that protects us.

A Sample Symbol Study: Ark of the Covenant

Shortly after God's chosen people left slavery in Egypt and began their travels toward the Promised Land of Canaan, God instructed them to make an ark—a boxlike container symbolic of God's presence—which they were to carry with them always. God further instructed the people to put within the ark the tablets on which Moses had inscribed the Ten Commandments under His divine inspiration. God's presence and His Word were to be inseparably linked before them.

Each Bible believer today is an ark of the covenant bearing the presence of God. Wherever we walk or travel, we are commanded by God to be carriers of His Word. We are to hide it in our hearts and carry it sealed within our spirits. We are to keep God's Word at the forefront of everything we do. We are to keep God's Word alive in our consciences, live by it, and enjoy God's presence. God's Word and His presence are inseparable in our lives, too.

Let's take the ark of the covenant as a symbol of

ourselves, devout believers on the earth. (See Exod. 37.)

- Wood = Our human nature
- Gold overlay = God's purity
- The inside of the box = Our unseen life
- The outside of the box = Our life visible to the world
- Lid (mercy seat) = The mercy of Jesus, who redeemed us through His death on the cross
- Seal = The Holy Spirit who seals our relationship with the Lord Jesus
- Crown = Our inheritance in Christ Jesus and a sign of our overcoming victory in Him
- Gold rings = God's love that links our "being" with our "doing" and ties all believers together in service to the Lord
- Staves = Ministries that carry God's power in us so that we reach the world
- Golden cherubim = Our guardian angels that protect us

Consider the three items inside the ark:

- Stone tablets = Our knowledge of God through the Old Testament
- Omer of manna = Our knowledge of the living Word of God, Jesus Christ (evident in the New Testament)
- Aaron's rod that bore fruit = The supernatural spoken word of God's Holy Spirit

50 ∙ Feasts in the Bible

God expects His people to rejoice and to enjoy life. The Bible describes many significant feast days. Every Jewish male was required to go up to the temple in Jerusalem for three feasts: Passover, Pentecost, and Tabernacles. Tabernacles was always to be a feast to which righteous Gentiles were invited.

You'll no doubt be amazed at the number of major biblical events that occur during feast and fast times. You'll also discover Jesus' participation in the feasts, what He taught about them, and His fulfillment of them.

Rosh Hashanah   The high holy days in Jerusalem begin with the New Year (Rosh Hashanah) on the first of the month of Tishri. Religious Jews go to the sea and symbolically throw their sins of the year into the sea of God's forgetfulness.

Feast of Trumpets   The Feast of Trumpets calls God's people to a new commitment of sacrificial giving and dedication to holy service (Tishri 1–3; see Num. 29:1–6).

Day of Atonement   The Day of Atonement (Yom Kippur) is on the tenth day of Tishri (see Lev. 23:26–32; Heb. 9:7). God set aside this day for continual repentance and prayers. It is a fast day rather than a feast day. It is the only day the Creator called a complete fast from sundown to nightfall the following day.

Feast of Tabernacles   The Feast of Tabernacles (Sukkoth) is described in Nehemiah 8:13–18, Zech. 14:16, and John 7:2. It is to last for seven days (Tishri 15–22)—a pure celebration of the tender keeping of the Lord. The eighth day is the height of joy, the Feast of Rejoicing in the Word (Simchat Torah).

The Feast of Tabernacles is to be a glorious time with singing, dancing, feasting, giving, and thanking the Almighty for provision, protection, and direction in individual lives. The Scriptures say these days are to be without worry, fear, anger, or concern.

Passover (Unleavened Bread)   This seven-day feast (Nisan 14–21) is held in the spring to commemorate the deliverance of God's people from Egypt; Jesus was crucified during this feast, symbolic of His sacrifice for our deliverance from sin. Our Christian celebration of Easter arose from the Jewish celebration of Passover. (See especially Exod. 12:43—13:10; Matt. 26:17–20.)

Pentecost (Firstfruits; Weeks)   This feast (Sivan 6) comes fifty days after Passover and recalls the giving of the Law to Moses on tablets of stone; it also represents the outpouring of a new law of love engraved on the hearts of believers by the Holy Spirit. The day of Pentecost is considered to be the birthday of the Christian church. (See especially Deut. 16:9–12; Acts 2.)

Sabbath   Every Sabbath is considered a time of feasting and rejoicing, a day in which God commanded worshipful rest for the spiritual, physical, and creative rejuvenation of His people. The Jewish Sabbath begins Friday at the setting of the sun and goes to nightfall on Saturday. (After Jesus' resurrection on the first day of the week, Christians began to meet together for worship on Sundays.)

Other Feasts   Other notable feasts are Purim (Esth. 9:18–21) and Hanukkah or the Festival of Lights (John 10:22). Our celebration of Christmas arose from the tradition of Hanukkah. In His love, God established these festival times during the year to bring needed refreshing to His children.

51 ▪ Seek the Text in the Original Language

Not one verse of the Bible was written originally in English. The Bible is a translation from another language and, in some cases, two or three translations.

For example, some translations of the Old Testament are based on the Septuagint, a Greek translation of the original Hebrew Scriptures. Jesus may well have delivered some of His major sermons in Aramaic or Hebrew. Both languages were common to northern Israel, and yet the New Testament was written mostly in Greek. As in the case of most translations, something of the richness and wit of the original language is invariably lost.

References   One way to recapture some of the missing texture is to consult a reference that expands the meaning of some words in the Bible. Here are several approaches you may take:

- Many Bibles have notes at the bottom of a page that elaborate on a concept or word. Take advantage of the helps already built into your volume of Scriptures.
- Both Greek and Hebrew lexicons have been placed in the back of *Strong's Concordance*.

These allow you to look up the "direct" word-for-word translation of each word in the concordance.

- *Hebrew Honey* by M. Countryman is a wonderful book that expands many concept words from the Old Testament.
- Much of Bible commentary work—for example, William Barclay's devotional commentaries on the New Testament—presents insights into the meaning of phrases and concepts in the original language.

In your Bible journal you may want to have a section for "Language Insights" in which you record what you learn about specific words or phrases.

If your interest in this area grows, many colleges, seminaries, and Bible colleges offer courses in biblical Hebrew and Greek that you may want to audit or take for credit. Although you won't come out of a sixteen-week course fluent in these languages, you will gain insights into the ways in which the original Bible languages are constructed and have a greater respect for the difficulties that scholars have faced down through the ages as they have attempted to translate the concepts of the Bible into other languages.

52 ■ Visit the Land of the Bible

A visit to Israel causes the Bible to come alive. In making a personal pilgrimage there, you will be able to

- walk where Jesus walked.
- visit the City of David.
- tramp over the remains of Solomon's stables.
- view the Valley of Armageddon.
- sail the Sea of Galilee.
- pause to read the beatitudes on a hillside next to the sea.
- have a picnic where Jesus fed the five thousand.
- walk through the gates of the Old City of Jerusalem.
- pray in the moonlight as you walk around the walls of the Old City.
- wade through Hezekiah's tunnel.
- visit the burial place Abraham bought and used for himself, Sarah, Isaac and Rebecca, and Jacob and Leah.
- pause to contemplate the death and resurrection of Jesus at the empty tomb.
- consecrate your life again at the Garden of Gethsemane.

- partake of Holy Communion on Mount Zion.
- worship the King of heaven on the Mount of Olives.

And there's so much more!

Many church groups arrange tours to the Holy Land. A trip to Israel is not as costly as a trip to many nations of the world. Most tours are priced around $160 a day, including airfare, hotels, and daily outings. Several study programs are available for college credit. They last about three to four weeks and cost about the same as a tour.

God's presence can be felt on His piece of real estate. To reach all the places we read about in the Scriptures takes only a few hours from New York. Plan a trip soon!

■ A Final Word

Have you started reading the Bible and feel as if you'll never understand it? Don't give up!

Keep reading!

Have you been reading the Bible regularly for some time and are feeling bored with your routine? Get out of the rut. Instead of reading your Bible at the regular time and place you have established, try reading it at another time and place.

Keep reading!

Have you read the same version all your life and feel as if you could quote certain passages in your sleep? Try a new version! Although it may seem "foreign" to you at the outset, you'll no doubt soon discover that you are gaining many new insights by seeing familiar passages packaged in new words and phrases.

Keep reading!

You'll never fully exhaust the fullness of God's Word, for God's Word bears God's nature. It is unchanging, everlasting, infinite, and all-wise. The good news is that we can grow in it, and through it, all of our lives. That's the best reason to . . .

Keep reading!